Books & My Food

THE IOWA

SZATHMÁRY CULINARY ARTS SERIES

Edited by David E. Schoonover

Literary
Quotations
and
Original Recipes
for
Every Day
in the Year

Elisabeth Luther Cary

and

Annie M. Jones

Foreword by David E. Schoonover

University of Iowa Press

Iowa City

ψ

Books & My Food

University of Iowa Press,
Iowa City 52242
Foreword copyright © 1997
by the University of Iowa Press
All rights reserved
Printed in the United States of America

http://www.uiowa.edu/~uipress

The recipes in this book have not been tested
by the publisher.

Printed on acid-free paper

Library of Congress Cataloging-in-Publication Data
Cary, Elisabeth Luther, 1867–1936.
Books and my food: literary quotations and original recipes
for every day in the year / by Elisabeth Luther Cary and
Annie M. Jones; foreword by David E. Schoonover.
p.   cm.—(Iowa Szathmáry culinary arts series)
Originally published New York: Rohde and Haskins, 1904.
Includes index.
ISBN 0-87745-604-6
1. Cookery.   2. Food—Quotations, maxims, etc.
3. Quotations.   I. Jones, Annie M.   II. Title.   III. Series.
TX714.C3732   1997
641.5—dc21   97-18489

97   98   99   00   01   02   C   5   4   3   2   1

FOREWORD

David E. Schoonover

IN her preface to *Books and My Food* (1904),
the American literary and art critic Elisabeth
Luther Cary declares that it is "impossible to
read English novels without realizing how important
a part food plays in the mental as in the physical life
of the Englishman." This literary/culinary daybook,
reissued for the first time in facsimile, provides a
food-related quotation accompanied by a recipe for
the foods mentioned, one pair for every day of the
year. The authors quoted are almost entirely Brit-
ish and mostly well known, although W. A. Crofful
and Jean Ingelow may not be household names now.
The group is predominantly male, with a sprinkling
of women present. Only Nathaniel Hawthorne and
Henry James represent the Americans.

Little is known about Cary's coauthor Annie M.
Jones, other than that she had published *Friends for
the Friendly: Quotations on Friendship* and *Homespun
Candies: Simple and Thoroughly Tested Recipes for Candy*

to Be Made at Home, both with the New York firm of Rohde and Haskins, in 1904. Cary and Jones were well prepared to serve up *Books and My Food* for the same publisher that year.

After 1908 Cary devoted most of her energy to serving as the first art critic of the *New York Times*, a post which no one individual had filled before then. Cary had received her general education solely at her home in Brooklyn from her father, Edward Cary, who was an editor of the *Brooklyn Union* and the *Times*. Both literature and art appealed to her. Her obituary in the *New York Herald Tribune* on July 14, 1936, stated: "Her first original book, *Alfred Tennyson: His Homes, His Friends and His Work*, was published in 1898. The next year she published *Robert Browning, Poet and Man* and, in 1900, *The Rosettis, Dante, Gabriel and Christina*. A work on William Morris was published in 1902 and one called *Ralph Waldo Emerson, Poet and Thinker* in 1904," the same year as *Books and My Food*. It went on to note that Cary "was the editor of *Poems of Dante Gabriel Rosetti*, published in 1903. In 1907 her *The Art of William Blake* and *Honore Daumier* appeared and, in 1908, *Artists, Past and Present*."

The *New York Times* obituary on July 14, 1936, described Cary as "A Noted Art Editor" who was "Known as [an] Authority in Her Field." She was extolled as "one of the most authoritative and widely known art critics in this country. For nearly thirty years her articles on many aspects of art, past and present, had appeared in *The New York Times*, revealing the point of view of a commentator exceptionally qualifed in her field, calmly unbiased amid controversy, and always alert to significant developments."

FOOD AND THE ARTS:
PAST, PRESENT, AND FUTURE

Interrelationships among food and the arts — literary, cinematic, painterly, musical — have existed for centuries but are more noticeable today than ever before. The University of Iowa Libraries and its Szathmáry Collection of Culinary Arts give a fair indication of the prevalence and range of topics on food and the arts. The Library of Congress has subject headings ranging from "Diners and Dining in Literature," "Gastronomy in Literature," "Cookery in Literature," and "Disorderly Eaters" to "Eating Disorders."

J. K. Hoyt's *The Romance of the Table (In Three Parts: I. Breakfast II. Dinner III. Tea)* (1872) certainly takes the form of culinary fiction, but the importance of food in books goes as far back as Homer. *The Thrill of the Grill* has no description tastier than this scene in *Iliad*, Book I: "The offerings destined to do honour to the god were quickly set in place round the well-built altar. . . . They . . . wrapped them in folds of fat and laid raw meat above them. . . . Young men gathered round . . . with five-pronged forks in their hands. When the thighs were burnt up and they had tasted the inner parts, they carved the rest into small pieces, pierced them with skewers, roasted them thoroughly, and drew them all off. Their work done and the meal prepared, they fell to with a good will on the feast, in which all had equal shares."

In *Odyssey*, Book VII, Odysseus speaks as a guest of Alcinous: "I would ask you now to let me eat. There is nothing more devoid of shame than the accursed belly; it thrusts itself upon a man's mind in spite of his afflictions, in spite of his inward grief. That is true of me; my heart is sad, but my belly keeps urging me to have food and drink, tries to blot out all the past from me; it says imperiously: 'Eat and be filled.'" Later, Odysseus, "having just cut a portion, rich in fat, from the chine of a white-tusked boar, sends it to the bard Demodocus, 'Let Demodocus have this dish to eat; I must do him this courtesy.'"

The Roman tradition would need to include Petronius Arbiter's *Trimalchio's Feast*, as well as Horace's *Epistles* and *Satires*. In *Epistles*, Book I, 1.5, Horace modestly states: "if you / Feel no dismay at a vegetable menu on crockery service, / I shall expect you, Torquatus, at *my* house for dinner at sundown. . . .

I undertake all appropriate functions as host very gladly." And in *Satires*, Book II, 2.8, Horace wonders: "What sort of time did you have at your dinner with rich Nasidienus?" Fundianus replies, "Starting us off was Lucanian boar, which the host said was captured / Under the sigh of a southerly breeze, and around it, for tangy / Garnish, were turnips and lettuce and radishes."

A small sampling of culinary scholarship would range from *The Loaded Table: Representations of Food in Roman Literature, Percorsi nelle Evidenze: Valenze Alimentari in "Pantagruel"* and *Tarte à la Crème: Comedy and Gastronomy in Molière's Theater* to *Jane Austen and Food* and *What Jane Austen Ate and Charles Dickens Knew.*

Culinary mysteries are either flourishing or bubbling over, according to different tastes: *Someone Is Killing the Great Chefs of Europe, The Nantucket Diet Murders, A Tasty Way to Die, Murder on the Menu, Dying for Chocolate, The Body in the Cast, Too Many Crooks Spoil the Broth, The Mid-Atlantic Mystery Cookbook,* and *Murder Most Delicious.* The subject of books and food reached some level of national awareness when it became the topic of a closing full-page feature in the *New York Times Book Review.* There, Walter Kendrick, a professor of English at Fordham University and the author of *The Secret Museum:*

Pornography in Modern Culture, let off his own steam on the issue in "Shut Up and Eat!"

In recent years a number of coffee-table books highlighting food and the painterly arts have included *Art What Thou Eat: Images of Food in American Art*, *Toulouse-Lautrec's Table*, *The Impressionists' Table*, and *The Sun & Moon Guide to Eating through Literature and Art*.

Since the famous eating scene in *Tom Jones* (the movie, 1963) aroused everyone's appetite(s), what might be labeled food films include *Babette's Feast*, *Eat Drink Man Woman*, *Like Water for Chocolate*, *My Dinner with Andre*, *Tampopo*, *Home for the Holidays*, *The Big Chill*, *Fried Green Tomatoes*, *Il Postino*, *Apollo 13*, *Leaving Las Vegas*, and *The Bridges of Madison County*.

In November 1996, a session of the Midwest Modern Language Association's annual program was devoted to "'Art What Thou Eat': Food in Literature, Art, and Culture," with four presenters, two from Romance language backgrounds and two from American literature backgrounds. The topics were "Feeding Fantasies: The Theatrics of Dining in the Spanish Theater of the Golden Age"; "You Are (Were) What You Eat: Food and Family in Ampara Davila's 'Alta Cocina'"; "'That Ever I Should Be Satisfied with Bread Again': Food as Pedagogy in Early American Women's Personal Narratives"; and "How to Eat, Drink, and Sleep as a Christian Should: Food, Gender, and Class in 19th-Century Domestic Serial Fiction."

When the Oxford Symposium on Food and Cookery convenes at St. Antony's College, Oxford (England) in 1998, the theme, chosen by a vote of some two hundred participating attendees in 1996, will be "Food and the Arts."

If Cary and Jones's *Books and My Food* was decades ahead of its time, it has a lively successor in Peg Bracken's 1976 *The I Hate to Cook Almanack: A Book of Days; Recipes & Relief for the Reluctant Cook and the Harried Houseperson.* Bracken seasons her almanac with a batch of real authors, ranging from Cleveland Amory to Dereck Williamson, and asserts that "all the people quoted in this book are real, though some are real only to me."

In *Books and My Food*, the compilers, authors, and recipes are real and ready to be enjoyed again by a new generation of readers with educated palates!

THE IOWA SZATHMÁRY
CULINARY ARTS SERIES

Many readers and collectors of cookbooks now agree with the *New York Times* that "Prose, Not Recipes,

Sells Today's Food Books" (May 15, 1991) and that "The History of Food [Has Gained] a Scholarly Pedigree" (May 30, 1984).

The cookbooks appearing in our series are selected from the University of Iowa Libraries' Szathmáry Collection of Culinary Arts, which contains more than 20,000 items: printed books dating from 1499 to 1996, more than 100 culinary manuscripts, some 3,500 ephemeral pamphlets and booklets, and a selection of professional and popular magazines.

The Szathmáry Collection is an extraordinarily varied trove, presenting more than five hundred years' worth of books and manuscripts on all aspects of food and its history. Our series provides today's readers and collectors with much more than recipes. Many of these cookbooks contain introductions, literary or historical matter, period advertisements, or a variety of illustrations that are interesting in themselves. The cultural context of cookbooks is also important — who prepared or published them, for what audience, in what time period?

Royalties from sales of volumes in the series assist the University of Iowa Libraries in purchasing books to enhance the Szathmáry Collection of Culinary Arts. The next volume, *The Receiptes Booke of Lady Borlase of Bockmore*, edited from the earliest English culinary manuscript in our collection, opens with a title page stating: "The receiptes within this booke were written by Robert Godfrey Servaunt to the right honble the Ladie Borlase of Bockmore in ye Parrish of Medmenham in ye county of Bucks in ye yeare of our Lord God one thousand six hundred sixty-five and in ye Seaventeenth yeare of King Charles ye Second over England."

ACKNOWLEDGMENTS

I would like to express my appreciation to these colleagues at the University of Iowa Libraries for their encouragement and assistance with this volume: Sheila Creth, Edward Shreeves, Robert McCown, Susan Hansen, Ann Ford, Lissa Lord, and Helen Ryan.

IN MEMORIAM
CHEF LOUIS SZATHMÁRY, 1919–1996

The Szathmáry Collection of Culinary Arts was gathered by Louis Szathmáry over a period of more than forty years, while "Chef Louis" owned and operated the Bakery Restaurant on North Lincoln Avenue in Chicago. In his busy — not spare — time, Louis wrote *The Chef's Secret Cook Book*, *Sears Gourmet Cooking Forum*, *American Gastronomy*, *The Chef's*

New Secret Cook Book, and *The Bakery Restaurant Cook Book* and edited the fifteen-volume series *Cookery America*. He also worked as a food consultant to major corporations and NASA, lecturer, newspaper columnist, radio broadcaster, collector, and generous donor. Louis passed away after a brief illness in Chicago on October 11, 1996.

PREFACE

Elisabeth Luther Cary

IT is impossible to read English novels without realizing how important a part food plays in the mental as in the physical life of the Englishman. The sentimental Anglo-Saxon soul goes out to its roast beef and pudding, to its port and ale, with much the same greeting it gives to its blue violets and Devon cowslips. The associations that cluster about especial dishes are not lightly to be dismissed. Perhaps no writer of another nation could have produced a poem difficult for the least emotional to read without tears, the theme of which should be a favorite soup at a famous restaurant. And if some of us have inherited from transcendental ancestors a species of contempt toward this gross and material affection for the food that gives us life, shares our nationality, and is the intimate of our homes, we may profitably remember the spirit of domesticity and hospitality which makes such an affection possible. It was before Emerson's second and longer visit to

England that he wrote against our being the "friends of our friend's buttons." Before he returned from that memorable second visit he wrote to his wife that if an Englishman were to visit her she must build a fire in the guest room and give him bread and wine at bedtime, for should an Englishman go cold, he said, it would chill his own bones, and, should he be hungry, he himself would be hungry all his life, so great had been the hospitality of the English toward him.

In making up this collection of recipes suggested by quotations chiefly from English novelists and poets, our idea has been not to provide Bohemian fare for our readers, or give them unfamiliar and unrelishable diet, but to show what a varied list might be gathered from the works of well-known writers, of dishes most of them equally well-known, and all of them good if properly prepared. The recipes for the more characteristically English cookery are taken from English sources. One little cook-book, undated, but apparently more than a century old, has furnished some excellent recipes, not one of which has failed in the trying.

We cannot do better than send out this result of what may seem to the serious-minded a somewhat whimsical effort to combine intellectual and bodily sustenance, with Stevenson's envoy to "Underwoods."

"Go, little book, and wish to all
Flowers in the garden, meat in the hall."

Books & My Food

JANUARY 1st

"The wedding-cake, which had been a great distress to him, was all eaten up. His own stomach could bear nothing rich, and he could never believe other people to be different than himself."—JANE AUSTEN ("Emma").

ALTHOUGH wedding-cake can hardly be recommended to invalids, I once heard of its curing a severe attack of indigestion, a statement the verification of which I leave to the skeptical. The following rule has descended from generation to generation of a long-lived family:

Twelve eggs, one pound of butter, one pound of flour, one pound of citron, three pounds of raisins, three pounds of currants, a pound and a half of brown sugar, a pint of molasses, half a pint of brandy, a teaspoonful of saleratus, one ounce of mace, one ounce of cinnamon, half an ounce of cloves, a quarter of an ounce of allspice, two grated nutmegs. Cook four hours in a slow oven, covering the top with paper after the first hour.

JANUARY 2D

"Lobster patties, rissoles, and two things with French names."—CHARLES READE ("It Is Never Too Late To Mend").

LOBSTER alone is good, but lobster with mushrooms is the perfect union of harmonious flavors. Cut the lobster meat into small pieces (do not chop it). Cut six large mushrooms into quarters. Dust them with paprika and salt, and pour on them a glass of sherry. Make a rich cream sauce of butter, flour, and cream (not milk). After it thickens, put in the pieces of lobster and mushroom, and pour in the sherry from which they have been taken, after they have cooked half an hour in the cream sauce. Do not allow the mixture to boil after adding the sherry. Pour it into hot patty shells and serve at once.

JANUARY 3D

"That vin de madère which accompanied the potage à la bisque would have contented an American."
—LORD LYTTON ("Parisians").

FOR an oyster bisque that would content even a Parisian, add to a quart of chicken stock a stalk of celery, an onion, and a dozen clams.

Cook until the celery is very tender, then strain and add to the stock a pint of milk and a pint of cream, both heated. Thicken with a tablespoonful of butter and two of flour rubbed together, and season with salt and paprika. Ten minutes before serving add thirty-five oysters and let them merely cook through.

JANUARY 4TH

"Well, that is intelligible," said Lady Selina Farrell, looking at her neighbor, as she crumbled her dinner-roll.—MRS. HUMPHRY WARD ("Marcella").

DINNER-ROLLS are made as follows: Add to a pint of milk, scalded and cooled, a tablespoonful of melted butter, a teaspoonful of salt, half a cake of compressed yeast dissolved in a very little lukewarm water, and six cups of flour. Mix into a sponge and cover. When light, pull off pieces about the size of a large egg, knead each of these into a smooth ball, then roll between the palms of the hands into a long roll about the size of a finger. Place close together in a biscuit pan and when light bake fifteen minutes in a hot oven.

3

JANUARY 5TH

"Dost think because thou art virtuous there shall be no more cakes and ale?"—SHAKESPEARE ("Twelfth Night").

FOR good little nut-cakes cream half a cupful of butter and a cup and a half of sugar; add the yolks of two eggs and beat all together. Sift two cupfuls of flour into which has been stirred a teaspoonful and a half of baking powder. Add to the butter, sugar, and eggs a cupful of milk, and then the flour. At the last stir in a cupful of chopped pecan or hickory nuts, and fold in lightly the whites of the eggs, beaten to a stiff froth. Bake in patty pan, ice and sprinkle chopped nuts thickly over the icing.

JANUARY 6TH

"Said he, 'Upon this dainty cod
How bravely I shall sup.'"
—HOOD ("Poems").

CROQUETTES of salt codfish are a pleasant variation of the familiar codfish cake. Make a thick cream sauce. Stir into it a pound of salt codfish shredded with the fingers after it has soaked two hours in warm water. Add a dash of red pepper. Do not cook the fish and the sauce, but allow the mixture to get cold and firm. Then shape into croquettes, dip each in beaten eggs, then in fine cracker-crumbs, and fry in very hot fat.

JANUARY 7TH

" Do daily soups
Your dinners introduce?"—GAY.

THE stand-by for soup is a simple consommé which may be multitudinously varied. Cut up two pounds of lean raw meat, beef or veal, and add a cupful of cold roast beef cut in pieces. Put over the fire with a cracked knuckle of veal, four quarts of cold water, two onions, one carrot, two stalks of celery, six peppercorns, a spoonful of salt, six cloves, and a few herbs. Cook slowly all day. Strain and when cold skim off the fat. Add the white and shell of two eggs. Bring to a boil and boil ten minutes. Strain through a cloth.

JANUARY 8TH

"Mrs. Elton was growing impatient to name the day, and settle with Mr. Weston as to pigeon-pies and cold lamb."—JANE AUSTEN ("Emma").

FOR an excellent pigeon-pie for a small family singe and draw three birds, split them down the back, wipe with a clean cloth, but do not wash. Fry half a dozen slices of salt pork and brown the pigeons in the pork-fat. Then put them into a deep baking-dish, slice a small onion, brown in the hot fat and add a pint of stock and a tablespoonful of flour. Stir until slightly thick, then strain over the pigeons. Cover them tightly and cook for two hours in a moderate oven. Remove the cover and replace it with one of pie-crust. Bake until brown.

JANUARY 9TH

"The mushrooms show his wit."—POPE.

FOR the large, highly-flavored and substantial mushrooms there is no better way of cooking than to broil them. Carefully wash, peel, and dry the mushrooms; pour over them a little melted butter, not hot, and put

them on ice for twenty minutes. When
chilled, broil upon an oyster broiler, first
on one side and then turn. About ten
minutes should be sufficient to cook
them. Serve upon delicately toasted
bread; season the last thing with salt
and pepper, a few drops of lemon-juice,
and a bit of butter on each mushroom.

JANUARY 10TH

"Mrs. Alexander Trott sat down to a fried sole,
maintenon cutlet, Madeira, and sundries."—CHARLES
DICKENS ("Sketches by Boz").

IF you ask for sole in the American
market you will get flounder; but
the mode of preparation is the same
for both. To fry the fish acceptably,
first scrape it, cut off the head and fins,
wash in cold water, and wipe dry.
Sprinkle with salt, dip twice in beaten
egg and bread-crumbs, and fry brown
in boiling lard or dripping. Serve with
it on a separate dish a mayonnaise dressing in which a tablespoonful of capers
has been stirred. For frying fish a pan
of deep fat and a frying basket are desirable. Butter should not be used, and
oil is better than lard or drippings.

"Of all the dishes that the ingenuity of man has invented, the truffled turkey or capon is the most delicious. On this point there is no difference of opinion."—DR. AUSTIN FLINT ("Essays").

DR. FLINT has not only given the weight of his authority to truffled turkey as a gastronomic delicacy, but has given a valuable suggestion as to its preparation. "It is not sufficient merely to fill a turkey with truffles and cook it," he says, "the art is to disseminate the flavor throughout the muscular tissue of the bird. The truffles should be of the best quality; they should be carefully prepared and seasoned; and the bird should be stuffed for days before it is cooked. In this way the truffle has a fair chance." He further adds that so admirable a dish as the wild turkey of this country, *truffé,* should be complimented by having the preceding dishes arranged with special reference to it, that the palate may not be cloyed with ordinary flavors before reaching it.

JANUARY 12TH

"An olive, capers, or some better salad."—BEN
JONSON.

NOTHING is better than celery
salad. Cut fine white celery into
lengths of an inch and a half or
two inches, splitting the ends, so that,
when thrown into ice-water for half an
hour they will curl back; when ready to
use mix with the celery a large table-
spoon of mayonnaise dressing, heap
lightly in a salad-bowl and put over the
top more of the mayonnaise through
which has been stirred a tablespoonful
of capers. A border of stoned olives or
pimolas is not only an attractive garnish,
but an improvement to the flavor.

JANUARY 13TH

"Butter ill melted—that commonest of kitchen
failures—puts me beside my tenor."—CHARLES
LAMB.

MELTED butter, or "Butter
Sauce" for fish is made by melting in a saucepan one tablespoonful of good butter, and as it melts
stirring in the same quantity of flour.
When thoroughly blended pour in a

9

cup of boiling water. Season with a saltspoonful of salt, a dash of pepper, a few drops of onion-juice, a pinch of made English mustard, a teaspoonful each of capers and minced cucumber pickle, and finally add slowly a well beaten egg. As soon as the egg is all in, take from the fire.

JANUARY 14TH

"There was a large, substantial, cold boiled leg of mutton, at the bottom of the table, shaking like blanc-mange."—CHARLES DICKENS ("Sketches by Boz").

FOR chocolate blanc-mange take half a package of gelatine dissolved in a cupful of cold water, stir into it a pint of hot milk (half milk and half cream is better), and a scant half cup of sugar; add four heaping tablespoonfuls of chocolate rubbed smooth with a little milk. Stir over the fire until the mixture is about to boil; when nearly cold flavor with a teaspoonful of vanilla and turn into a mould wet with cold water. A boiled custard or whipped cream served with this is a decided improvement.

JANUARY 15TH

"A little strong gravy soup lubricated and gelatinized with a little tapioca."—CHARLES READE
("It Is Never Too Late To Mend").

IF you have three-quarters of an
hour's notice to make an emergency
soup you can have one answering
the above description. Cook in a quart
of boiling water a cupful of pearl tapioca; dissolve in a cup of hot water half
a dozen bouillon capsules or an equal
amount of beef extract; strain and add
to the tapioca with a cupful of canned
tomatoes, a little chopped onion; season
rather highly; put into the tureen small
squares of bread browned in the oven.
Some cooks also put into the tureen a
well-beaten egg and on this pour the
hot soup.

JANUARY 16TH

"Then came a dish of meat—nature unknown, but
supposed to be miscellaneous—singularly chopped
up with crumbs of bread, seasoned uniquely though
not unpleasantly, and baked in a mould."—CHAR-
LOTTE BRONTË ("Shirley").

AN old way of making "English
meat pie" is to take finely chopped
cold beef, put in a deep baking
dish a layer of the meat, strew lightly

with bread-crumbs, season highly with salt, pepper, butter, and a few drops of onion-juice; repeat the process till the dish is full or your meat used up. Pour over it a cup of stock or gravy, or, lacking these, hot water with a teaspoonful of butter melted in it; on top a good layer of bread-crumbs should be put, seasoned and dotted with butter. Cover and bake half an hour; remove the cover and brown.

JANUARY 17TH

"At this moment Mrs. Hayes' servant appeared with a smoking dish of bacon and greens."—THACK-ERAY ("Catherine").

A NOVEL but very desirable variation on the old dish of bacon and greens is often served in one household to the approval of family and guest. Carefully prepare and cook spinach in the usual way, season it with salt, pepper, and two or three table-spoonfuls of cream, or rather less of butter, after you have drained and chopped it. Fry very crisp thin slices of bacon and lay thickly over the dish of spinach. The combination is appetizing.

JANUARY 18TH

"Old Stella placed a cold fowl upon the table, and followed with a savory omelette."—HAW-THORNE ("The Marble Faun").

FOR a winter morning there is no better omelette than one made savory with sausage, which should be partly cooked, skinned, if the sausage links are used, and minced fine. Then break and lightly beat to six eggs. Have a small tablespoonful of butter hot in a pan, slip in the eggs, shake gently in one direction. When set add the minced sausage; fold the omelette and serve without delay.

JANUARY 19TH

"At the top a fried liver and bacon were seen, At the bottom was tripe in swinging tureen."
—GOLDSMITH.

DIP thin slices of bacon in ice-water, then put in a hot pan; when it begins to curl add two or three slices of onion and cook two or three minutes longer, being careful that the bacon does not get too hard. Take out the bacon and keep hot; remove the onion from the pan and lay in the slices of liver which have been seasoned with salt and pepper and dredged with flour; cook rather slowly till brown and tender. Too rapid cooking dries and hardens it. Lay the liver on a dish with the bacon, stir into the gravy a tablespoonful of butter rubbed to as much brown flour; season with tomato catsup or stewed tomatoes. Pour over the liver.

JANUARY 20TH

"It was he who proposed the bowl of punch, which was brewed and drunk in Mrs. Betty's room, and which Gumbo concocted with exquisite skill."
—THACKERAY ("The Virginians").

FOR rum punch take two large fresh lemons with rough skins and some lumps of sugar. Rub the sugar over the lemons until it has absorbed all the yellow part of the skins. Then put into the bowl these lumps and as many more as the lemons will probably require. Squeeze the lemon-juice on the sugar, and blend sugar and juice thoroughly together. Much of the excellence of the punch depends upon the mixing processes being well performed. Add two quarts of boiling water and stir until almost cool. Then add from one pint to one quart of rum as the punch is desired weak or strong. Mix again very thoroughly.

JANUARY 21ST

"Bless the girls! a nice fresh steak was frizzling on the gridiron for our supper."—THACKERAY ("The Fatal Boots").

USE a hip-bone steak. Have the bone cut entirely out, and the steak pressed together to form a round slice. It should be at least two inches thick. Cook over a clear fire seven minutes to a side. This will give a very rare steak. When done place on a hot platter and cut three or four deep gashes in one side. Fill the gashes with a dressing made of four teaspoonfuls of French mustard, two or three drops of tabasco sauce, a small teaspoonful of salt, and butter the size of an egg. Do this quickly that the steak may not have time to cool, and send to the table at once.

JANUARY 22D

"Leek to the Welsh, to Dutchmen butter's dear,
Of Irish swains potato is the cheer."
—GAY ("Poem").

NO "Irish swain," but a clever Frenchman invented the potato soufflé. To a well-beaten cupful of mashed potato add the yolks of three eggs, thoroughly beaten; season with salt and pepper and a tablespoonful of melted butter. Whip in slowly a cup of milk, or half milk and half cream, and finally the frothed whites of the eggs. Put into a baking-dish and cover till it rises well, then remove the cover and brown. Serve at once or it will fall.

JANUARY 23D

"Take the nuts from the fire with the dog's foot."
—TAYLOR.

TO blanch and salt almonds put them into boiling water and let them stand five minutes; then throw them into cold water and rub off the loosened skin. Put in a bowl, allowing to each cupful of nuts a tablespoonful of olive-oil or melted butter. Stir the almonds that they may be well coated; let them stand for an hour, then sprinkle with salt, a dessertspoonful for each cupful of the nuts; spread on a baking-pan and put into a moderately hot oven. Let them cook for about fifteen minutes, stirring several times that they may brown evenly. Take them out when they are a delicate brown.

JANUARY 24TH

"I never was much of an oyster eater, nor can I relish them *in naturalibus* as some do, but require a quantity of sauces, lemons, cayenne peppers, bread and butter, and so forth, to render them palatable."—THACKERAY ("The Fitzboodle Papers").

MANY people accustomed to the ordinary oyster of commerce secretly agree with Thackeray, hence the popularity of the oyster cocktail. The "sauces, peppers, and so forth," are frequently overdone, however, a simple mixture bringing out the flavor of the oyster instead of destroying it. The following is acceptable to a moderately initiated palate:

To six oysters add the juice of half a lemon, two drops of tabasco-sauce, two teaspoonfuls of *home-made* catsup,

and the oyster-juice. Place the mixture
where it will be thoroughly chilled, but
do not put ice into it. Some people like
a teaspoonful of horse-radish added, but
this coarsens the flavor.

JANUARY 25TH

"Wo'ld ye have fresh cheese and cream?"—
HERRICK ("Poems").

AN old-fashioned method of serving pot-cheese still obtains in one
family where ancient traditions
are still held in special honor.

Mix a pot-cheese with rich cream
enough to make it soft, add to it a tablespoonful of chopped Spanish onion.
Season with a liberal sprinkling of red
pepper and eat *sans peur et sans re-
proche.*

JANUARY 26TH

"There were great round, pot-bellied baskets
of chestnuts, shaped like the waistcoats of jolly
old gentlemen."—CHARLES DICKENS ("Christmas
Carol").

TO make the peculiarly luscious
dessert known as nesselrode
pudding you must boil three cupfuls of these jolly old gentlemen;

when tender remove their shells and brown skins and mash them into a pulp. Cut a pound of French candied fruit into small pieces and pour over them a glassful of sherry. Mix a cupful of water with two cupfuls of sugar and boil fifteen minutes. Into this syrup stir the beaten yolks of four eggs. Return it to the fire and let it reach the boiling point, then remove and beat it until it is cold. Add a pint of whipped cream, the nuts, fruit and wine and a teaspoonful of vanilla. Freeze in an ice-cream freezer, then pack and leave for two or three hours.

JANUARY 27TH

"Bearing, in one hand, a most enormous sandwich, while in the other he supported a goodly sized case bottle, to both of which he applied himself with intense relish."—CHARLES DICKENS "Pickwick Papers").

A "CLUB SANDWICH" has a roystering sound to the feminine ear, but in reality its composition is of the daintiest: Two thin slices of delicately browned toast; between them a thin slice of carefully broiled ham, the fat crisp and brown; a thicker slice from the breast of chicken, and a lettuce-leaf touched with mayonnaise.

JANUARY 28TH

"Among the viands were expected to be found a small assortment of cheese-cakes and tarts."—CHARLOTTE BRONTË ("Shirley").

FOR cheese-cakes make a pie-crust of half a cup of butter, two cups of flour and a tablespoonful of ice-water. Roll out very thin, rolling into the dough half a cup of grated cheese, preferably old English; cut into fancy shapes, sprinkle with grated cheese and bake in a quick oven till a delicate brown.

JANUARY 29TH

" 'Hippocrates and Galen,' he cried, ''tis a soupe au vin,—the restorative of restoratives.' "—CHARLES READE ("The Cloister and the Hearth").

FOR a *soupe au vin* it is only necessary to take a good consommé and when ready to heat for use put in it a dozen whole cloves, as many whole allspice and a few pieces of cinnamon tied in a thin muslin bag. When ready to pour into the tureen remove the spice-bag and add a cupful of port or Madeira wine. If neither of these wines is at hand, sherry will answer, though not quite as good for the purpose.

JANUARY 30TH

"Feed him with apricots and dewberries, with purple grapes, green figs."—SHAKESPEARE ("Midsummer Night's Dream").

FOR a delicate fig pudding, choose good pulled figs, soak over night in enough claret to cover them; in the morning simmer gently on the side of the range, adding enough claret to take the place of that absorbed by the figs, sweeten very slightly; let them cook till the skins are tender, set away to cool and serve covered with whipped cream sweetened and flavored with sherry. A few candied cherries on the cream add both to the flavor and appearance of this good and unusual dessert, but are not necessary.

JANUARY 31ST

"Simplicity talks of pies."—WILLIS ("Love in a Cottage").

A RICH lemon-pie sadly unfitted for a cottage income is made by creaming half a pound of butter with a pound of sugar, beating in the yolks of six eggs, the juice and grated peel of two lemons, a gill of brandy, and the whites of four eggs previously whipped stiff. Bake with a bottom crust only. When done cover with a meringue made of the whites of two eggs, two tablespoonfuls of sugar and a little lemon-juice. Return to the oven until the meringue is a very light brown. Eat cold the day it is baked.

FEBRUARY 1ST

"Well saffroned was that barley soup."—ROBERT BROWNING ("Ferishtah's Fancies").

BOIL two pounds of lean veal in one quart of water, add to it one quarter of a pound of pearl barley and boil until it can be rubbed through a sieve, add a quart of warm milk or white stock, bring to the boiling point, season with salt and serve. This is a very nourishing soup or purée.

FEBRUARY 2D

"Now if you're ready, Oysters, dear, we can begin to feed!"—LEWIS CARROLL ("Through the Looking Glass").

TO prepare oysters for frying, choose small, fat ones of good flavor in place of those larger and more tasteless. Drain, wipe, and dip each one in highly seasoned cracker-crumbs, then in beaten egg and again in the crumbs. Set away for an hour or more in a cold place. Fry a few at a time, in boiling lard.

FEBRUARY 3D

" A pair of boiled fowls, with tongue and et ceteras, were displayed at the top, and a fillet of veal at the bottom."—CHARLES DICKENS (" Sketches by Boz ").

FOR fricasseed chicken cut two fowls into joints. Season them with salt and pepper and dip each one in flour. Put them in a saucepan and cover with boiling water. Let them cook very gently for about two hours, or until very tender. When they are done put three tablespoonfuls of butter in a frying-pan, add the same amount of flour, rub smooth, then add the water in which the chickens have been boiled, which should not amount to more than a quart. After the gravy has boiled up add a cup of rich cream and season with salt, white pepper, and a little cayenne. Just before removing from the fire add an egg well beaten. Pour over the chicken, which should be laid on toast or soda biscuits cut in half.

" 'Tom,' said Maggie, as they sat on the boughs of the elder-tree, eating their jam puffs, 'shall you run away to-morrow?' "—GEORGE ELIOT ("Mill on the Floss ").

PUFF-PASTE, that bugbear of the inexperienced cook, is in reality easy of accomplishment. Chop three-quarters of a cup of butter into a pint of sifted flour, having the ingredients and the chopping-bowl thoroughly chilled. Pour in half a cup of ice-water and mix with the chopping-knife to a stiff paste. Turn out on a floured pastry-board and roll quickly into a thin sheet. Dredge with flour, dot with lard, fold in three thicknesses and roll out again. Repeat the process three times, then set the sheet of paste in the ice-box near the ice over night. In the morning divide it into as many pieces as you wish to have pies and roll each piece to fit the pie-plate. For "Jam Puffs" fill with jam after baking.

FEBRUARY 5TH

"We have five eggs. No meat for you, dear, but enough bread and butter, some honey and plenty of coffee."—GEORGE MEREDITH ("The Amazing Marriage").

BOILED eggs with cream sauce make an excellent breakfast dish. Boil the eggs hard; remove the shell and cut in halves; put in a warm covered dish and pour over them a sauce made by heating a cupful and a half of milk (part cream is better), stirring into it two tablespoonfuls of butter and one of flour rubbed together; season with salt and paprika and cook for ten minutes, until thick and smooth. A teaspoonful of curry powder added to the sauce is an improvement or a piece of onion cooked in the butter may be used as a flavoring.

FEBRUARY 6TH

"That gentleman had in his hand a cabbage. He was proving to the farmer that this plant is more nutritious than the potato."—CHARLES READE ("Clouds and Sunshine").

IF the gentleman had argued thus of cauliflower, which has been called a "cabbage with a college education," he would have been quite correct, for in cultivation the cauliflower has gained in nutritive importance. Boil in salted hot water till tender, but not soft. Divide the "flowers," put in a buttered dish a layer of the cauliflower seasoned with salt, pepper and butter, then a sprinkling of grated cheese and one of bread-crumbs. Moisten with milk each layer, end with a layer of dry bread-crumbs liberally dotted with butter. Cover and bake for half an hour, then remove the cover and brown.

FEBRUARY 7TH

"The mustard is too hot a little."—SHAKESPEARE ("Taming of the Shrew").

FOR those who find the English mustard moistened simply with vinegar too hot and crude, a very pleasant condiment may be made by rubbing into two tablespoonfuls of the ground mustard a tablespoonful of olive-oil, a saltspoonful each of celery salt and black pepper, a teaspoonful each of salt and sugar, and enough vinegar to make it of the right consistency to pour. For some tastes, it is an improvement to rub the bowl in which the ingredients are mixed with onion or garlic.

FEBRUARY 8TH

"Betty Jay scented the boiling of Squire Cass's hams."—GEORGE ELIOT ("Silas Marner").

THE rules for the simplest dishes are often the hardest to find in cook-books. The right way to boil a ham is simplicity itself. Soak the ham all night after scrubbing it hard with a stiff brush kept for the purpose. Boil in a' soup "digester" if possible, as such a vessel admits of cooking at a slow, even temperature. Start it in cold water, and after it comes to the boiling point put the kettle back where it will simmer gently. Fifteen minutes to a pound is the length of time usually given for the boiling, but an eight-pound ham really requires at least four hours of slow boiling to reach the perfection of tenderness. When it is done either allow it to stand twenty-four hours in the water before skinning it, or skin it as soon as it is cooked, sprinkle it over with brown sugar, stick into it a few whole cloves at sparse intervals and bake in a hot oven until nicely brown. Serve with a champagne-sauce, which is merely a good brown sauce flavored with a glass of champagne. It is delicious to eat hot.

FEBRUARY 9TH

"The venosta ran on in praise of Paris and the Parisians, of Louirer and his soirée and the pistachio ice."—LORD LYTTON ("Parisians").

A SIMPLE ice-cream is made of one quart of cream, half a pint (or more) of milk, one cup of sugar, and a tablespoonful of vanilla extract. Scald the cream and milk, add the sugar and when cold, the flavoring, one-half cup of pistachio nuts and a quarter of a cup of almonds, blanched, chopped and pounded to a paste. Freeze.

FEBRUARY 10TH

"Set your mind on curly fat rashers of bacon and sweetly smelling coffee, toast, hot cakes, marmalade and damson jam."—GEORGE MEREDITH ("The Egoist").

V ERY good and quickly made hot cakes are prepared by beating one egg very light, stirring in a cupful of flour, half a cupful of milk and two tablespoonfuls of sugar, beating them briskly till light and then stirring in quickly a good teaspoonful of baking-powder. Bake in muffin tins for twenty minutes in a quick oven. This will be enough for half a dozen muffins.

FEBRUARY 11TH

"What had ye till your dinner?"
"I forget."
"A choep likely?"
"I think it was."—CHARLES READE ("Peg Woffington").

WHEN the broiler is unavailable and the chafing-dish or frying-pan must serve your need for cooking chops, you will feel no regrets if you heat the pan very hot, then put in a lump of butter, about a tablespoonful for four chops; when the butter is melted add the chops, nicely trimmed; cover and cook two minutes, turn them, season with salt and butter, and when they are a light golden brown they are done to perfection. This will be in four or five minutes.

FEBRUARY 12TH

"And salmon—perhaps salmon is next to the flounder."—THACKERAY.

A SALMON-LOAF is a "dressy" dish to set before a lunch party, and may be made the preceding day. Pick cold salmon into flakes, mix two cupfuls with the yolks of two hard-boiled eggs, a tablespoonful of minced parsley, two of lemon-juice, and one of capers. Season highly. Pour a cupful of veal or chicken stock (heated) over half a box of gelatine; stir in the fish. Decorate a buttered mould with slices of egg and olives, pour in the mixture and let it get perfectly cold. Garnish with lettuce-leaves.

FEBRUARY 13TH

"Moore eats like three men; they are always making sago or tapioca or something good for him."—CHARLOTTE BRONTË ("Shirley").

TO make a delicious sago-cream soak a cupful of sago in two cups of cold water till it takes up all the water. Scald a quart of milk and stir the sago into it. Remove from the fire to do it. When almost cold beat it all up from the bottom, stir in two tablespoonfuls of sugar creamed with one of butter and the yolks of five eggs. When well mixed add the whipped whites of the eggs. Pour into small moulds, bake and eat cold with soft custard or wine sauce.

FEBRUARY 14TH

"The *Last of Lent* was spunging upon Shrovetide's pancakes."—CHARLES LAMB.

TO make the regular Shrovetide pancakes soak in a quart of milk two cupfuls of dry bread-crumbs, free from crusts; when the crumbs are thoroughly moistened beat in three eggs whipped light, a tablespoonful of melted butter, a teaspoonful of salt, and a table-spoonful of sugar. When well mixed stir in half a cupful of twice-sifted flour in which is mixed half a teaspoonful of baking-powder. Cook on a hot, lightly greased griddle and serve with butter and sugar and ground cinnamon.

FEBRUARY 15TH

"First catch your clams; along the ebbing edges
Of saline coves you'll find the precious wedges."
—W. A. CROFFUL.

FOR a delicate but very good clam-chowder take one pint of clam-juice, forty clams chopped very fine, eight potatoes, peeled, parboiled, and chopped into coarse pieces; two small onions, sliced: one quart of toma-toes; cook all together for three hours, then add half a cup of butter and a cup of flour rubbed together, and a quart of milk. Cook half an hour longer. The addition of a bunch of celery, chopped fine, improves the flavor.

This makes a large quantity, and half the amounts given will be enough for eight persons.

FEBRUARY 16TH

"I am a great eater of beef, and I believe that does harm to my wit."—SHAKESPEARE ("Twelfth Night").

MOST English people are great eaters of beef and cook it in a large variety of ways. A beefsteak pie is better known across the water than here. It should be made of cold broiled beefsteak cut in thin slices across the grain. If any bit of the outside is burned, discard it, as it will make the whole dish bitter. Sprinkle the pieces of beef with flour, pepper, and salt, add a chopped onion and two cupfuls of gravy made of melted butter, flour and water (the flour rubbed smoothly into the butter and boiling water added). Bake in a pudding-dish with a biscuit-crust.

FEBRUARY 17TH

"My lord, I hope you are pepper proof."—SWIFT.

CUT off the stem ends of sweet green peppers and remove the seeds. Stuff with a mince of tongue, veal, chicken, or lamb, mixed with an equal quantity of bread-crumbs, and seasoned with salt, butter, and a bit of onion-juice or tomato. Put the peppers close enough together in baking-dish so that they will stand upright. Cover the bottom of the dish with stock, or water enriched with a large spoonful of butter.. Cook in a moderate oven for an hour. Remove and add flour and butter to the liquid in the pan. Pour over the peppers and serve.

FEBRUARY 18TH

"There is a physiognomical character in the taste for food. C— holds that a man cannot have a pure mind who refuses apple-dumplings."
—CHARLES LAMB.

TO make boiled apple-dumplings pare tart apples of good flavor and remove the cores; fill the holes with butter, sugar, and a little cinnamon. Have ready a dough made of two tablespoonfuls of butter chopped into

33

a quart of sifted flour, in which has been well mixed a heaping teaspoonful of baking-powder and a little salt; wet with two cupfuls of milk, to make a soft dough, and roll to a thickness of a quarter of an inch. Cut into squares large enough to readily encase the apples; put an apple in each and fold together, pinching the edges tight. Tie up in small cloths, not too tight, and boil an hour, never allowing the water to stop boiling.

FEBRUARY 19TH

"The greengrocer and his wife then arranged upon the table a boiled leg of mutton, hot, with caper sauce, turnips and potatoes."—CHARLES DICKENS ("Pickwick Papers").

WITH turnips and boiled leg of mutton it is well to serve a dish of browned potatoes. Cut into strips of convenient size six cold mashed potatoes. Dip first into melted butter and then into beaten egg. Lay the strips carefully in a buttered pan; cook in a hot oven for twelve minutes.

FEBRUARY 20TH

"I had to eat boiled mutton every day: *entre nous*, I abominated it. But I never complained. I swallowed it."—THACKERAY ("Roundabout Papers").

IF mutton must be boiled it should be served rare. Put it into a kettle of water that is boiling hard, and cook fast for fifteen minutes to keep the juices in the meat. Then draw the kettle to one side of the range and let the contents cook slowly ten minutes to the pound of meat. Add to the liquor a stalk of celery, a minced onion, a sprig of parsley, chopped, a sprig of mint, and a carrot. When the meat is taken up it should be washed over with butter. Strain the stock, season with salt and pepper, thicken with flour, stir in a lump of butter and a tablespoonful of capers, and serve as gravy.

FEBRUARY 21ST

"Some bring a capon, some a rurall cake,
Some nuts, some apples; some that thinke they make
The better cheeses, bring 'hem."—BEN JONSON.

NUTS and cheese have recently become a favorite combination. Form cream cheese into small balls and press half a walnut-meat on each side, first seasoning the cheese with a little paprika or with chopped green pepper. Arrange the balls on lettuce-leaves or else on the tender white central leaves of the chicory-plant. Garnish with shredded red peppers and olives, and pour a French dressing over all.

FEBRUARY 22D

"She sent him for a pie she professed to have fallen in love with at the corner of the street."—CHARLES READE ("Peg Woffington").

ONE of the several kinds of cake known as "Washington pie" is made by creaming together half a cupful of butter and two cupfuls of sugar, adding the beaten yolks of four eggs and a cupful of water, beating well together and stirring in three cupfuls of flour in which has been mixed two teaspoonfuls of baking-powder. At the last flavor with the grated rind of a lemon and a little nutmeg and fold in the whites of the eggs. Bake in layers. Put together with a filling made of the yolk of an egg beaten up with a cupful of sugar, the grated peel and juice of a lemon, and three tart apples, grated. Cook in a double boiler till scalding hot, stirring constantly. When cold put between the layers of cake. It is excellent eaten fresh.

FEBRUARY 23D

"Give him three ratafias soaked in a dessert-spoonful of cream."—GEORGE ELIOT ("Mill on the Floss").

RATAFIA is a cordial made by blanching two ounces of peach and apricot kernels, bruising them and putting them in a bottle with a pint of brandy. Set it aside for a month, then remove the kernels and add a cup of cold water in which has been dissolved half a pound of sugar, strain through a cloth and seal. George Eliot's little ratafias are no doubt named for the custom of dipping macaroons or other small cakes in this liqueur and serving them with custard.

FEBRUARY 24TH

"By the way, we had half-a-dozen sardines while the dinner was getting ready, eating them with delicious bread and butter."—THACKERAY ("Memorials of Gormandising").

A PARTICULARLY delicious method of preparing sardines is to rub half a dozen of them to a paste with the yolks of three hard-boiled eggs. Season with lemon-juice. Place on squares of delicately toasted white bread, garnishing with watercress, which is the best of green salads to eat with sardines.

FEBRUARY 25TH

"So long as there's pickled pork in the kitchen, they'll look in."—CHARLES READE ("Propria Quae Maribus").

FOR the occasions when an old-fashioned breakfast of fried mush is in demand, with its traditional accompaniment of fried pork, cut the slices of fat pork very thin; pour hot water over them, drain, plunge in ice-water for a couple of minutes and fry in a hot pan till crisp; or they may be rolled in egg and crumbs and fried in deep fat.

FEBRUARY 26TH

"It was a memorable feast. I had soup, fish, meat and pastry, and, for the first time in my life, a glass of wine."—GEORGE MEREDITH ("Harry Richmond").

TO convert the commonplace cod-fish or halibut steak into a rather distinguished dish, the New Orleans method is to fry the steaks in oil, or part butter and part lard; before they are quite done take them out and add to the gravy in the pan two tablespoonfuls of flour, one of Worcestershire sauce, some ground cloves, nutmeg, half an onion, minced, and a little thyme. Strain into it also half a pint of stewed tomatoes; stir well, and when thoroughly blended put in the fish and cook all together for three or four minutes and serve immediately.

FEBRUARY 27TH

"If you will but speak the word, I will make you a good Syllabub."—WALTON ("Complete Angler").

THE famous syllabub of Walton's native Staffordshire was a lusty English product as different from our airy nothings as were his simple rods and lines from the modern equipment of fancy rods and magnificent flies. It was made by putting into a bowl a pint of cider and a glass of brandy, a little nutmeg and sugar, and then pouring into it from some height a pint of warm milk.

FEBRUARY 28TH

"Give him a sugar-plum if he is good."—CHAR-
LOTTE BRONTË ("Shirley").

AN easy and very good "sugar-
plum" to make at home requires
one can of sweet condensed milk,
one and a half cupfuls of brown sugar,
a large tablespoonful of butter, a teaspoonful of vanilla and half a pound of
English walnuts. Boil twenty minutes,
stirring steadily; pour on buttered plates
and when nearly cold cut in squares.

MARCH 1ST

"At private houses what does one get now?
—*blanc de poulet*—flavourless trash!"—BULWER
("Parisians").

POTAGE *à la Reine,* which is one
form of the despised "blanc de
poulet," is sufficiently delicious for
any festival occasion. Remove the fat
from a quart of chicken-broth; season
with salt, pepper, and a little onion, and
put on to boil. Soak in a little milk half
a small loaf of bread-crumbs and mix
with them the yolks of three hard-boiled
eggs, mash smooth, chop the white meat
of a boiled chicken to a powder and
stir it into the bread-crumbs and eggs.

Stir in slowly one pint of hot cream and mix with the hot chicken-broth. Boil five minutes; if too thick add more cream; if not thick enough, more crumbs. The white meat of cold roast chicken may be used.

MARCH 2D

"Turbot with capers is the thing. The brisk little capers relieve the dulness of the turbot; the melted butter is rich, bland and calm."—THACKERAY ("Memorials of Gormandising").

THIS fish is fortunate in being the better for keeping a day or so, when so many kinds of fish need absolute freshness to make them palatable. Soak the turbot in salted water for at least half an hour before cooking, put it into a pan of boiling water in which are the juice of two lemons and two tablespoonfuls of salt. Put the black side of the fish down when the water begins to boil, skim and set back where it will only simmer for half an · hour. At the end of that time drain it carefully, place on a platter covered with a napkin, garnish with parsley, lemon and hard-boiled eggs and serve with white sauce to which capers have been added. A six-pound turbot is a good size.

MARCH 3D

"Here's a pigeon so finely roasted, it cries, Come, eat me!"—Swift ("Polite Conversation").

IT is only a very tender pigeon which can be confident of its roasted charms, but the right bird is delicious so cooked. Draw, wash and wipe; pepper and salt the insides; tie into shape or fasten with skewers; wrap the birds with slices of fat bacon or salt pork, and put in the pan with half a cup of hot water to which a teaspoonful of butter has been added. Cook for fifteen minutes before removing the bacon, then rub with lemon-juice and butter and brown. Put the pigeons where they will keep hot while you stir into the gravy a table-spoonful of butter rubbed into one of browned flour. Boil up once.

MARCH 4TH

"Some cheeses are made of skimmed milk and some o' new milk, and it's no matter what you call 'em, you may tell which is which by the look and the smell."—George Eliot ("Adam Bede").

TO make fresh pot-cheese place in rather a shallow pan milk that has turned a little sour, put it over a sauce-pan of boiling water and heat almost to the boiling point. After about six minutes turn the milk over by spoonfuls, to heat it all equally. When heated through, turn into a collander to drain; when free of whey, add salt to taste and butter. A few spoonfuls of cream improves it.

MARCH 5TH

"Thy child as surely grasps an orange as he fails to grasp the sun."—ROBERT BROWNING ("Ferishtah's Fancies").

PARE sweet seedless oranges, take off the inner tough white covering and divide into sections. Add to the beaten whites of two eggs two tablespoonfuls of cold water. Dip the sections of orange in it and then roll each one in granulated sugar. Put on a platter the sections, not touching; set in a warm oven for three or four minutes, then set away to cool.

MARCH 6TH

"Presently, we were aware of an odour gradually coming towards us, something musky, fiery, savoury, mysterious,—a hot drowsy smell, that lulls the senses, and yet enflames them,—the *truffles* were coming."—THACKERAY ("Memorials of Gormandising").

IF I remember rightly, Thackeray was in France when he wrote of truffles. Certainly in no other country do they correspond to his description. The way to realize a faint reminiscence of the reality is to buy a can of French pâte de foie gras of the best make procurable, spread the contents on thin strips of toasted bread, and eat them as gaily as the occasion warrants. Do not insult the memory Thackeray has enshrined by pretending that the canned truffle of the grocery is the delicacy to which he refers.

MARCH 7TH

"For Miss Barker had ordered all sorts of good things for supper—scalloped oysters, potted lobsters, jelly, a dish called ' little Cupids.'"—GASKELL ("Cranford").

SCALLOPED oysters are somewhat uncertain unless a good rule is carefully followed. This one has always produced admirable results.

44

Drain the oysters and do not use the liquor. Cover the bottom of a buttered dish with a layer of oysters, place on this a layer of fine bread-crumbs (not cracker-crumbs), over which dabs of butter and plenty of salt and pepper have been˙ strewn. Then another layer of oysters, until the dish is full, with a layer of crumbs on top. Moisten with a cup of milk, slightly thickened. Bake half an hour.

MARCH 8TH

"Well, eat and be thankful!" says the Little Sister, who was as gay as a little sister could be, and who had prepared a beautiful bread sauce for the fowl." —THACKERAY ("The Adventures of Philip").

TIE a chicken that has been cleaned but not stuffed into a piece of cheese-cloth. Plunge it into a kettle of boiling water to which a table-spoonful of vinegar has been added. Let it simmer until tender—twenty minutes to the pound ought to be enough. Unwrap and serve with bread-sauce.

Rule for sauce: Pour a quart of hot milk in which an onion has been boiled tender, over two cupfuls of stale white bread (grated). Let it stand an hour, then turn the mixture into a sauce-pan, add butter the size of an egg mixed with

two tablespoonfuls of flour, boil for five
minutes, season with salt and pepper.

MARCH 9TH

"It was Mrs. Gill as I have seen her, making
custards in the heat of summer in the cool dairy,
with rose-trees and nasturtiums about the latticed
window, preparing a cold collation for the rectors
—preserves and 'dulcet creams.'"—CHARLOTTE
BRONTË ("Shirley").

"**D**ULCET creams," warranted to
please the most fastidious of
rectors, are made with two
dozen almonds, blanched and pounded
and boiled in a little milk, the yolks of
five eggs beaten well, a wine-glass of the
best brandy, a teacupful of sugar and a
quart of cream. Set over the fire and
bring to the boiling point, stirring until
it thickens, pour into glass cups and serve
cold.

MARCH 10TH

"On the plain household bread his eye did not
dwell; but he surveyed with favor some currant
tea-cakes, and condescended to make choice of
one."—CHARLOTTE BRONTË ("Shirley").

CURRANT jumbles still give delight to children (and to grown-
up children as well), as an accompaniment to a cup of afternoon tea.

Beat a cupful of butter to a cream, then beat in two cupfuls of sugar and add two well beaten eggs, and, finally, three scant cupfuls of flour in which have been stirred two heaping teaspoonfuls of baking-powder and half a teaspoonful of salt. The dough should be stiff enough to roll thin. Sprinkle the tops of the jumbles with currants and peanuts chopped fine and a little granulated sugar. Ten minutes in the oven is generally enough to bake them.

MARCH 11TH

"Give cherries in time of year, or apricots; and say they were sent you from the country."—BEN JONSON.

FROZEN apricots can be given any time of year by using fruit that has been canned or preserved. Cut in very small pieces one can of apricots, add a quart of water and two cups of sugar and freeze. When partly frozen add two-thirds of a cup of cream, whipped to lightness. Stir into the apricot and finish freezing. If the apricots used are preserved, less sugar will be needed, but all frozen desserts need more sugar than unfrozen ones.

MARCH 12TH

"If you are hungry, can't you be content with the wholesome roots of the earth?"—SHERIDAN ("The Duenna").

FEW people realize the excellent flavor of celery-root. Cut it in thin slices and boil for about two hours, or until tender. Serve with a cream sauce. It will have a much stronger flavor than the stalk of the celery, and possesses even more valuable attributes as the calmer of irritated nerves.

MARCH 13TH

"The pie dishes were now drawn out of the ashes and broken, and the meat baked with all its juices was greedily devoured. 'It tastes like a rabbit.'"—CHARLES READE ("It Is Never Too Late To Mend").

ADD to one pound of lean chopped beef one-quarter of a pound of bacon; season highly with salt and pepper, and, if the flavor is liked, with one teaspoonful of minced onion; stir into it a beaten egg, and form into a long roll. Incase in a shell of buttered paper and place in a pan; cover closely the whole with a thick paste of corn-meal. Bake three-quarters of an hour;

remove the paste and serve. If it does not taste like a rabbit it will at least taste much better than an inferior cut of steak, which costs nearly twice as much.

MARCH 14TH

"Twice meat was forbidden and twice pudding allowed."—MRS. HUMPHRY WARD ("Marcella").

AN excellent rule for custard pudding is this: beat until very light the yolks of six eggs and seven tablespoonfuls of sugar. Pour slowly on them a quart of hot milk, in which is a small pinch of salt; fill buttered custard-cups with the mixture, set in a pan of hot water and bake until set, then draw to the door of the oven and quickly dot the surface of each custard with currant-jelly, raspberry-jam or other favorite and convenient substitute; cover with a meringue made of the whites of three eggs and a tablespoonful and a half of powdered sugar. Brown lightly.

MARCH 15TH

"Better a crust of black bread than a mountain of paper confections."—ARTHUR HUGH CLOUGH ("The Bothie of Tober-na-Vuolich").

OLD-TIME New England brown bread is almost as sweet and nutty as a confection. To make it, sift two cupfuls of rye flour, two cupfuls of Indian meal, two teaspoonfuls of salt and one of soda, dissolved in a little hot water. Mix into a white bread sponge that is already light and add gradually half a cup of molasses. Knead well and leave six or seven hours. Then knead into loaves and let rise for two hours longer. Bake three hours in a slow oven.

MARCH 16TH

"Papa was great at lobster salads and taught me. I mixed it myself a fortnight ago, and, as you see, it is as fresh and sweet as if I had just made it."
—GEORGE DU MAURIER ("Peter Ibbetson").

A BOILED salad dressing that does keep "fresh and sweet" for a fortnight is made by adding three tablespoonfuls of vinegar to the beaten yolks of three eggs, heating in a double-boiler and stirring until stiff. On removing from the fire stir in two tablespoonfuls of butter, mixing thoroughly. Season when cold with salt, mustard, and cayenne, and thin with olive-oil to the desired consistency. Keep in a cool place.

MARCH 17TH

"For the first course at the top, a pig, and pruin-sauce."—GOLDSMITH ("She Stoops to Conquer").

PRUNES, to be eaten with meat, should not be sweetened. Soak a pound of carefully washed prunes in cold water over night. Put them into a stew-pan with a quart of fresh water, and two lemons that have been cut into thin slices, from which the seeds have been removed. Let them simmer gently for three hours. Serve cold. They are to be eaten with pork, veal or duck, in place of the sour apple-sauce usually served.

MARCH 18TH

"Shall we pay respect to this haunch, Mr. Quin?" —CHARLES READE ("Peg Woffington").

A HAUNCH of mutton cooked with care gives a change from the leg and chops which are the usual winter resource. It should not be used till it has hung some time. Rub it well with vinegar several times the day before cooking it, when it should be covered with a thick paste of flour and water and cooked in a very slow oven for several hours. Three-quarters of an hour before eating it the paste should be removed and the mutton basted often. There will not be much gravy in the roasting-pan, so a brown or stock gravy should be made to serve with it. This should give a juicy roast. Currant jelly should be passed with roast mutton.

MARCH 19TH

"Dear Mrs. B— Chops and tomato-sauce. Yours, Pickwick."—CHARLES DICKENS ("Pickwick Papers").

TOMATO-SAUCE with more flavor than that usually served with chops is made by adding to one quart of canned tomatoes a chopped onion fried in a little butter and two cupfuls of strong brown soup, highly seasoned with salt and pepper. Cook for three hours on the side of the range. Strain through a purée-sieve. Return to the stove and thicken with a tablespoonful of flour rubbed into an equal quantity of butter.

MARCH 20TH

"The meat o' the meal folk made some fifty years ago."—BROWNING ("Fifine at the Fair").

THIS is one of Browning's abstruse utterances which we might refer to the Browning Societies. In the meantime we may assume that meat o' the meal is plain flour, and may be used in making a flour-soup, which is better than its name sounds. Brown a tablespoonful of flour in the same quantity of melted butter. Pour into it a pint of milk and bring to the boil. Season with salt, red-pepper and parsley. After taking it from the fire stir through it the beaten yolk of an egg. A teaspoonful of onion-juice may be added if liked.

MARCH 21ST

"Do you put cayenne into your cream-tarts in India, sir?"—THACKERAY ("Vanity Fair").

CAYENNE cannot be recommended as a flavoring for cream-tarts, but preserved ginger can be. Bake in round patty-pans a plain pie-crust dough till a light golden brown. When cold pour into the pie-crust shells a cream made by stirring into a cup and a half of boiling milk two-thirds of a cup of sugar, two eggs, beaten lightly, whites and yolks together, and two tablespoonfuls of flour, made smooth with cold milk; a pinch of salt should be added when the cream has cooked for fifteen minutes and two tablespoonfuls of preserved or candied ginger, chopped fine. Put on each tart a small round of the pastry.

MARCH 22D

"Mrs. Bates, let me propose your venturing on one of these eggs. An egg boiled very soft is not unwholesome. Serle understands boiling an egg better than anybody . . . you need not be afraid, they are very small, you see—one of our small eggs will not hurt you."—JANE AUSTEN ("Emma").

EVEN Mr. Woodhouse would have found eggs boiled in the following manner wholesome. "Serle" herself could not have improved upon it. Cover the eggs with boiling water, allow them to boil one minute, then move back to where the water remains at the boiling point but does not actually simmer. In five minutes remove from the fire, when the whites and yolks will be cooked to a jelly-like consistency, but not hardened.

54

MARCH 23D

"And, Frances, lass, I brought some cresses in:
Just wash them, toast the bacon, break some eggs."
—JEAN INGELOW ("Poems").

BACON may be very delicately prepared for an invalid (or a well person!) by chilling in iced-water before broiling over a brisk fire. When partly cooked remove quickly from the fire, plunge the pieces again in iced-water, shake the water off and return to the broiler. Serve very hot, with cresses fresh from the brook and you have a dainty rural breakfast.

MARCH 24TH

"I eat my apples, relish what is ripe."—ROBERT
BROWNING ("Ferishtah's Fancies").

INTO a tablespoonful of hot butter stir two tablespoonfuls of flour, and when it begins to thicken pour in two cupfuls of scalded milk in which has been dissolved a quarter of a teaspoonful of soda; stir for two minutes and add the yolks of four eggs, beaten light; then stir in six large pippins, pared and grated, and, when they have been well mixed, the whites of the eggs, beaten stiff. Half fill buttered custard or popover cups, set in a pan of hot water and bake in a quick oven until they puff up and are sufficiently brown. Open the oven door and let them dry for a couple of minutes. Brandy or lemon-sauce should be served with them.

MARCH 25TH

"There were ruddy, brown-faced, broad-girthed Spanish onions, shining in the fatness of their growth like Spanish friars."—CHARLES DICKENS ("Christmas Carol").

PEEL and parboil Spanish onions for a few minutes; drain and let them stand till quite cold. Take out the centre from each and stuff with a mixture of finely chopped cold meat, ham, chicken or veal, and one-third as much fine bread-crumbs. Season with salt, paprika, and bits of butter. Set the onions close together in a dish with a little stock, or gravy. Sprinkle well with bread-crumbs and bake about half an hour.

MARCH 26TH

"Patties of lobster and almonds mixed."—
CHARLES READE ("The Cloister and the Hearth").

FILL puff paste patty shells with a mixture compounded of two cupfuls of lobster cut in small pieces and a half cupful of blanched and chopped almonds, stirred into two cupfuls of cream, to which has been added the beaten yolks of two eggs and a glass of sherry. Let the cream, eggs, and wine cook together in a sauce-pan over boiling water until the cream begins to thicken; season with half a teaspoonful of salt and a little paprika, add the lobster and nuts, boil, then fill the patty shells. Almond-meal may be used to thicken the cream, in place of the nuts.

MARCH 27TH

"My good old Aunt, who never parted from me at the end of a holiday without stuffing a sweetmeat or some nice thing into my pocket, had dismissed me one evening with a smoking plum-cake fresh from the oven."—CHARLES LAMB ("Essays of Elia").

"A SMOKING plum-cake," such as boys like, is no more than a soft ginger-bread with raisins stirred in. Make as follows: Mix a batter of one cupful of butter, one cupful of New Orleans molasses, one cupful of sugar, one cupful of sour milk or buttermilk, one teaspoonful of soda, dissolved in a little boiling water, a tablespoonful of ground ginger, a teaspoonful of cinnamon, two eggs and about five cupfuls of flour; reserve one cupful of flour to dredge two cupfuls of seeded raisins to be added at the last. Bake in a moderate oven, thirty to forty minutes.

MARCH 28TH

"Gerard took out his pudding and found it delicious."—CHARLES READE ("The Cloister and the Hearth").

"GERARD'S brown-bread pudding" is made with half a pound of stale brown bread, grated, the same amount of currants and raisins, four eggs, half a pound of shredded suet, a gill of cream, a cup of sugar, a teaspoonful of nutmeg and a small glassful of brandy. Boil in a floured cloth one hour. This is a very light and delicate pudding, by reason of omitting the flour, usually considered necessary.

MARCH 29TH

" 'Art is very well,' said Mr. Brandon, ' but with such pretty natural objects before you I wonder you were not content to think of them.'
" 'Do you mean the mashed potatoes, Sir?' said Andrea, wondering."—THACKERAY ("Diary of C. Jeames de la Pluche, Esq.").

MASH six large, freshly boiled potatoes with an open wire masher to keep them light and flaky. Season with a tablespoonful of butter; salt and pepper to taste. Stir in a cupful of cream; beat into them two eggs. When well beaten, heap lightly in the dish in which they are to be served and set in the oven until a rich golden brown.

MARCH 30TH

"And you, gentlemen, what do you say to some iligant divvled kidneys for yourselves?"—THACKERAY ("The Tremendous Adventures of Major Gahagan").

SCALD a beef kidney, skin and slice it in thin slices, put an ounce of butter into a frying-pan; when hot add the kidney, a tablespoonful of Worcestershire sauce, a saltspoonful of salt, a teaspoonful of dry mustard, simmer five minutes, add a gill of sour wine. Move the pan back and forth for a few moments over the fire, then serve.

MARCH 31ST

"He takes mutton chops for dinner and the best of arrow-root for supper."—CHARLOTTE BRONTË ("Shirley").

WHEN you would have arrow-root for supper put into a sauce-pan half a pint of water, a glass of sherry, or a tablespoonful of brandy, a little grated nutmeg and a scant tablespoonful of sugar. Let it boil up once, then stir in a dessertspoonful of arrowroot, previously rubbed smooth, with two spoonfuls of cold water. Return to the fire, stir and boil three minutes.

APRIL 1ST

"This Bouillebaisse a noble dish is—
  A sort of soup or broth, or brew,
Or hotch-potch of all sorts of fishes,
  That Greenwich never could outdo:
Green herbs, red peppers, mussels, saffron,
  Soles, onions, garlic, roach and dace:
All these you'll eat at *Terré's* tavern
  In that one dish of Bouillebaisse."
                    —THACKERAY ("Poems").

THE famous bouillebaisse is indeed, as Thackeray describes it, a sort of fish chowder, but it seldom contains all the ingredients he mentions. It may be made with four pounds of fresh cod, two onions, a clove of garlic, one peppercorn, two stalks of celery, a quart of white potatoes cut in small pieces, salt, pepper, and a quarter of a pound of salt pork, cut in slices. Put all the ingredients together in a granite kettle and stew slowly in water enough to cover them for three or four hours. Just before serving add one quart of hot milk.

APRIL 2D

"Invite him to dinner, Emma, and help him to the best of the fish and chicken, but leave him to choose his own wife."—JANE AUSTEN ("Emma").

SHAD seems to the English visitor the best of American fish, and the truly national way of cooking it is to plank it—a much simpler operation than it is commonly regarded. A shad plank may be bought now at any large housefurnishing store. Split the fish as for broiling, wash and wipe dry, and tie with the inside upward on the plank. Salt and pepper thoroughly and dredge with flour. Either place the plank before a grate of clear coals—the orthodox way—or in a very hot oven. A thick shad will take fully half an hour to cook. When done, cut away the cords and butter the fish well, serving it on the plank.

APRIL 3D

"A little pipkin with a bit
Of mutton or of veal in it,
Set on my table trouble-free,
More than a feast contenteth me."
—HERRICK ("Poems").

TO prepare a knuckle of veal, cut all the meat from the bone, which should have been broken in several places. Put the bones in a pint of cold water and bring slowly to the boiling point. Remove the sinews from the meat which you have cut off. Put a tablespoonful of butter in the bottom of a kettle and let it melt. Dredge flour, salt, and pepper over the pieces of veal and put them in the kettle to brown, stirring them for four or five minutes till they are delicately colored. Add a small carrot, one onion, and a bit of parsley. Pour over the browned veal the bones and the water in which they have been cooking, which should be boiling hot by this time. Cover closely and allow to simmer about three hours. When it is done remove the veal and vegetables, take out the bones, thicken the gravy with a tablespoonful of flour, taste and see if more seasoning is desirable. If you have mushrooms, two tablespoonfuls, cut in pieces, will be an addition. Pour over the veal and serve.

APRIL 4TH

"Give me a piece of marchpane."—SHAKESPEARE
("Romeo and Juliet").

BLANCH a pound of Jordan almonds and pound them in a mortar almost to a powder, add to them three-quarters of a pound of confectioners' sugar and stir in a few drops of orange-flavor water; beat all together until it becomes a good paste; dust a little fine sugar on the rolling-board and roll the paste, shaping it as you please; ice by brushing with fine sugar wet with rose-water or orange-water, and bake in a moderate oven.

APRIL 5TH

" 'Very astonishing indeed! Strange thing!'
   Turning the dumplings round, rejoined the King."
                    —WOLCOTT.

DUMPLINGS to serve with veal stew will be beautifully tender and light if the following directions are observed. Mix one pint of flour, half a teaspoonful of salt, two teaspoonfuls of baking-powder and a teacupful of milk into a soft dough. Pull off bits of the dough and drop into the stew while it is boiling. Cover the stew-pan tight and do not uncover for ten minutes, when the dumplings should be done. Then serve immediately.

APRIL 6TH

"Quite ready for the fowl and mashed potatoes, Sir?"—CHARLES DICKENS ("The Haunted Man").

THE flavor of a baked potato is always superior to that of the b o i l e d Friend-of-the-Irishman. A touch of elegance is added by cutting off the tops of the potatoes after they are baked, scooping out the inside, beating it up with butter, salt and cream, until smooth and light, returning it to the shells, and browning in the oven.

APRIL 7TH

" A paté of fruit conserved after a receipt devised by Gerard Moore's 'grand'mere' . . . completed the dinner." — CHARLOTTE BRONTË ("Shirley").

CHOP a small teacupful each of apple, orange, candied lemon-peel, and Sultana raisins. Add a wine-glass of sherry, half a teaspoonful of powdered cloves, a tablespoonful of brandy, and a teacupful of sugar. Fill patty-shells of thin puff-paste and bake half an hour in a moderate oven.

APRIL 8TH

"How sweet the butter our own hands have churned!"—CHARLES READE ("It Is Never Too Late To Mend").

THE small modern churns that come for "making butter while you wait" solve all difficulties in the way of having the fresh, sweet butter so much liked by many people, but no one need be deterred from having it by the lack of a churn, as the largest sized egg-beaters and a kitchen-bowl answer admirably. The cream needs to be heavy and it comes more quickly if it is near but not at the souring point. Beat briskly past the whipped-cream stage and the butter soon comes. No better butter can be made than has been produced with a bowl and a wooden paddle.

APRIL 9TH

"He heard the bacon sputter on the fork,
And heard his mother's step across the floor."
—JEAN INGELOW ("Poems").

HE might as easily have heard the bacon sputter in the frying-pan, if his mother had placed there half a dozen slices when the pan was hot. To make fried bacon delicious, remove, when beginning to curl up at the edges, to a hot dish, and fry half a pound of mushrooms, steamed, washed, and peeled, in the bacon fat left in the pan. Pour them over slices of toast, arrange over them the bacon and serve hot.

APRIL 10TH

"To feed on caviare and eat anchovies."—RAN-DOLPH ("Muse's Looking-Glass").

SPREAD on delicate slices of toast anchovies from which the heads and backbones have been taken: the best are those packed in bay leaves and spices. Lightly scramble five eggs, in which are stirred one large tablespoonful of butter, four of cream, salt and pepper. When the eggs begin to thicken turn on to the toast. A cupful of tomatoes cut in bits is an addition much liked by many, or stewed tomato may be used if more convenient.

APRIL 11TH

"The sweets shook and trembled, till it was quite impossible to help them." — CHARLES DICKENS ("Sketches by Boz").

FOR a pleasant and wholesome dessert, orange charlotte is well adapted. Soak one-third of a box of gelatine in a third of a cup of cold water; when dissolved pour on a third of a cup of boiling water, the juice of a large lemon and one cup of sugar. Strain and add a cup of orange-juice and pulp and a little of the grated rind. Cool in a pan of ice-water; when cold add a cup of cream whipped stiff. Line a mould with lady-fingers or stale cake and pour in the orange mixture.

APRIL 12TH

"A barn-door fowl
Which does not awe you with its claws and beak,
But which in cackling sets you thinking of
Your eggs to-morrow at breakfast, in the pause
Of finer meditation."
—MRS. BROWNING ("Aurora Leigh").

EGGS fried in sweet-oil make a pleasant variety and are more delicate than the usual fried egg. Put about two tablespoonfuls of olive-oil in a hot spider; when the oil is hot break in one egg, then another; by the time the second egg is in the pan the first will be ready to fold over. By the time the second is folded the first is ready to take out. Repeat until enough eggs are cooked.

APRIL 13TH

"This dish of meat is too good for any but anglers or very honest men."—ISAAK WALTON ("Complete Angler").

"KEBOBBED mutton" is a dish that would answer to the gentle angler's description. Remove all the fat from a loin of mutton and cut it into chops or steaks. Dip these into the yolks of three eggs and sprinkle over them bread-crumbs seasoned with salt and pepper and summer savory. Place them together as before they were cut and tie them in shape. Roast them in a quick oven half an hour, basting with butter and the juices of the meat. Make a gravy by adding to the liquid remaining in the pan after the meat is cooked a tablespoonful of flour and a teacupful of tomato catsup.

APRIL 14TH

"You'd find sandwiches and sherry in plenty if you were to search his carriage."—TROLLOPE ("Phineas Finn").

A DELICIOUS sandwich to eat with wine is made of Jordan almonds, pounded in a mortar, sprinkled with sugar, moistened with rich cream, and spread on thin slices of Boston brown bread.

APRIL 15TH

"These procure quiet sleep, violets; lettuce, especially boiled; syrup of dried roses; saffron; balm: apples, at our going to bed."—BACON.

PICK apart a head of lettuce, wash carefully, and put into a steamer over a kettle of boiling water (a steamer may be improvised by using an ordinary colander and a pot of boiling water), cover closely, laying a thick folded cloth upon the lid. Boil hard for half an hour, then drain and lay the lettuce leaves upon a hot dish; salt and pepper, and if this dish is not eaten at bedtime to "secure quiet sleep," it will be much improved by pouring over it a sauce piquant.

APRIL 16TH

"You can make whipt cream; pray what relief
Will that be to a sailor who wants beef?"
—W. KING.

WHILE whipped cream may well be considered too light and airy to satisfy a brawny sailor, it is quite substantial enough to follow the beef. Poured over marrons glacés, flavored with sherry or Madeira, and capped with a candied cherry, it will please both eye and palate.

APRIL 17TH

"Mrs. Jamieson was kindly indulgent to Miss Barker's want of knowledge of the customs of high life, and, to spare her feelings, eat three large pieces of seed-cake."—MRS. GASKELL ("Cranford").

THE economies of Cranford make it probable that Miss Barker's seed-cakes were concocted by a rule not unlike the following, which calls for cheap materials and produces a result likely to please a Jamieson palate:

Mix a quart of flour with half a pound of sugar and a quarter of an ounce of allspice; melt three-quarters of a pound of butter with half a pint of warm milk; add while warm a quarter of a yeast-cake and work up to a smooth dough, mixing into it a cupful of cleaned currants and half a cupful of caraway-seeds. Bake an hour and a half.

APRIL 18TH

"Tongue; well that's a very good thing when it ain't a woman's. Bread—knuckle o' ham, reg'lar picter—cold beef in slices, wery good."—CHARLES DICKENS ("Pickwick Papers").

BOIL corned tongue four hours, after soaking it over night, serve it hot with spinach cooked as follows: Clean the spinach thoroughly, rinsing in several waters, boil rapidly for half an hour (no water need be put in the pot). Drain and chop coarsely. Season with pepper, salt and butter.

APRIL 19TH

"Our country member, growing hot at cheese and salad time, about the spread of democracy in England, burst out as follows."—WILKIE COLLINS ("The Moonstone").

THE following combination of cheese and salad is good. To a cupful of cold chicken, or veal, add a cupful and a half of grated cheese. Make a dressing of the yolks of three hard-boiled eggs, rubbed smooth; stir in three tablespoonfuls of salad-oil, a teaspoonful of dry English mustard, or two of the German prepared mustard, a good sprinkling of paprika, half a teaspoonful of salt, and two tablespoonfuls of vinegar or three of lemon-juice. Mix with the cheese and chicken and garnish with the whites of the eggs.

APRIL 20TH

"The cooks are hard at work, Sir, chopping herbs and mincing meats and breaking marrow-bones."—CIBBER ("Love Makes a Man").

THE herb which we most use with meat—as well as drink—is the fragrant mint, and the sauce of that name is made by adding to four tablespoonfuls of vinegar three each of chopped mint and granulated sugar, crushed together, and a dash of white pepper. Serve cold.

APRIL 21ST

"She was good enough to give me some the other day with *soupe aux choux*."—ANNIE I. THACKERAY ("The Village on the Cliff").

FOR cabbage-soup of a delicate flavor pull apart and wash the cabbage-leaves, let them lie an hour or more in cold water; then put in a sauce-pan with enough boiling water to cover and a tablespoonful of salt. Cook for forty minutes, or until tender; drain off the water and chop fine. Put in a sauce-pan three tablespoonfuls of butter, two of flour, a stalk of celery, a bay-leaf, and a quart of white stock, or, in its absence, a quart of milk. Cook slowly for ten minutes, then remove the bay-leaf and celery, stirring till smooth; then add the cabbage, season with salt and pepper, cook ten minutes, stirring constantly. If it is desired to have a smooth soup, put through a sieve, otherwise add half a pint of cream and serve.

APRIL 22D

> " There stay thy haste
> And with the savoury fish
> Indulge thy taste."—GAY.

REDSNAPPER, firm of flesh, plump, and handsome, is a fish that deserves to be better known than it is. It is more delicious boiled than baked, as is also the case with shad, so rarely seen boiled, with its delicate flesh unimpaired in texture and flavor. There should be enough boiling water in the kettle to cover the fish. To a gallon of water add the juice of three lemons, half a teacupful of salt, and one of vinegar. After the fish is in the water bring quickly to a boil, then push the kettle back where the water will simmer gently. Cook from half to three quarters of an hour.

"The baddish boy chuckled, and addressed himself to the nice brown steaks with their rich gravy."
—CHARLES READE ("Christie Johnson").

THERE are steaks and steaks. Nearly every untrained applicant for a cook's situation declares that she can broil a steak and heat up canned tomatoes, but her steaks are not, as a rule, of the following type:

A cut from the first, second, or third rib of a roasting piece of beef, the bone removed, the steak rubbed with olive-oil, dusted with pepper, salt, and flour, and broiled over a charcoal fire, held near the hot coals for the first two minutes, then lifted up from them to complete the cooking more slowly. For a rich gravy to accompany it, mince fine two shallots, boil ten minutes in two gills of claret, add half a pint of strong brown stock and a pinch of cayenne pepper. Pour over the steak.

APRIL 24TH

"It was a very light, wholesome cake, Brown made it on purpose for the children."—THACKERAY ("The Newcomes").

BOIL together half a pint of water and two-thirds of a cup of butter. While boiling add two cups of flour even full. When cool add five eggs, well beaten. Drop on a pan. Bake in a quick oven twenty minutes. Put together with a layer of cream, or split and fill with cream.

Rule for cream: Boil one pint of milk, when boiling add two eggs, one cup of sugar, and half a cup of flour, beaten together. Boil two or three minutes, remove from the fire, stir in a small piece of butter, and a teaspoonful of vanilla flavoring.

APRIL 25TH

"Stay, John, did you perceive anything in my chocolate cup this morn?"—SHERIDAN ("St. Patrick's Day").

CHOCOLATE for immediate use should be made by dissolving in water one and a half ounces of sweet chocolate for each cup, stirring from time to time. It should be allowed to boil fifteen minutes to make it smooth and consistent. Serve with cream, whipped or plain.

Brillat Savarin quotes a good authority as saying that chocolate in perfection is made over night for breakfast, allowing it to remain on the side of the range and reheating when ready to serve.

APRIL 26TH

"Custards for supper, and an endless host
Of syllabubs and jellies and mince-pies,
And other such ladylike luxuries."
—SHELLEY.

DISSOLVE half a box of gelatine in half a pint of wine. Add one cupful of sugar, two beaten eggs, and one pint of cream, heated to the boiling point. When cool stir in another pint of cream, whipped stiff and flavored with grated orange-peel. Pour into a jelly-mould and place near the ice to set.

APRIL 27TH

"For meadow buds, I get a whiff,
Of Cheshire cheese, or only sniff,
The turtle made at Cuff's."—HOOD.

THERE are many ways of using the well-known Cheshire cheese, but a very good way is to pound four ounces of it with one ounce and a half of butter, a half teaspoonful of white powdered sugar, a little bit of mace, and a wine-glass of white wine. Press down into a jar.

APRIL 28TH

"Sweet turnips are the food of Blouzeind."— GAY.

"SWEET turnips," when they are young and tender, may be pared and cut crosswise in quarter-inch slices. Lay in ice-cold water for half an hour. Cook till tender in boiling unsalted water. Drain and dry on a cloth, and before they are quite cold sprinkle with pepper and salt, cover with flour and fry.

APRIL 29TH

"Deviled chicken and buttered toast."—DIS-RAELI ("Coningsby").

CUT cold chicken in inch squares, as nearly as possible. Cover with olive-oil and lemon-juice and stand them in a cold place for two or three hours; then season with pepper, salt, and a little dry mustard, dip in egg and cracker-crumbs and set aside till stiff, then fry a light brown. Have ready a cupful of good white sauce, allow it to boil up, then beat through it a table-spoonful of cream and an egg. Half fill ramakins with the chicken and pour into each some of the sauce.

APRIL 30TH

"Miss Bates, let Emma help you to a *little* bit of tart—a *very* little, little bit. . . . You need not be afraid of unwholesome preserves here."— JANE AUSTEN ("Emma").

TAKE the yolks of two eggs, the juice of two lemons, one cup of sugar, two even tablespoonfuls of flour and one half cupful of water. Bake with a bottom crust only, and when done cover with a meringue made of the whites of the eggs, beaten up with two tablespoonfuls of sugar and a little lemon-juice. Return to the oven until the meringue is a very light brown.

MAY 1ST

"I'll teach you to draw, you young dog!
Such pictures as I'm looking here at!
'Old Mounseer making soup of a frog'
There 'Palmam qui meruit ferat.'"
—HOOD ("Poems").

SKIN the hind legs of frogs and lay in milk for fifteen min-utes; stew in barely enough water to cover and cook till tender. Remove the meat from the bones and chop fine. Heat a quart of white stock made from chicken or veal; thicken with one tablespoonful of flour, rubbed into one of butter and half a teacupful of dry fine bread-crumbs; add the frog meat, allow it to boil for a minute or two, stir in a little chopped parsley; season with salt and pepper and it is ready to serve.

MAY 2D

"Old Tray licked all the oysters up,
  Puss never stood at crimps,
But munched the cod, and little kit
  Quite feasted on the shrimps."
            —HOOD ("Poems").

THE fresh shrimps when in market are to be preferred, but good canned ones in glass bottles may be obtained. To a pint of shrimps, when boiled and taken from the shells, allow a large cupful of milk; when it is hot add a tablespoonful of butter rubbed into one of flour. Stir until well blended, then put in the shrimps, season with salt and paprika. When ready to take from the fire, stir in a beaten egg.

If the canned shrimps are used be sure to rinse in cold water some minutes before using.

MAY 3D

"Of course we must have something to eat.
. . . There'll be a cutlet—on a trunk—anyway."
—Mrs. Humphry Ward ("Lady Rose's Daughter").

IF the cutlet was of veal it should have been thoroughly cooked, as underdone veal is proverbially unwholesome. To insure a tender, palatable and digestible veal cutlet prepare and cook it as follows: Season the meat with salt and pepper. Heat three tablespoonfuls of salad-oil very hot in a frying-pan. Fry the cutlet in this until brown on both sides. Pour off the oil and substitute a cupful of boiling water, a cupful of stewed tomatoes, and two dozen mushrooms. Cover the pan closely and let the meat simmer for an hour in the sauce.

MAY 4TH

"Those roots that shall first spring and be most delicate."—Shakespeare ("Henry V.").

YOUNG carrots are particularly nice prepared as follows Scrape the carrots, slice as thin as possible with a sharp knife; put into a sauce-pan with very hot butter, tossing them with a knife to prevent sticking. Cook till they begin to brown and are done through, which will be in a few minutes. Season well with salt and pepper, pouring the melted butter over them. Each ring of the carrot has a different flavor, and cooking in this way blends them best.

MAY 5TH

"Tea and cake on the table—beauty seated by his side,—all in less than a minute. He offered her a piece of cake 'Na! I am no for any.' He replied by putting a bit to her heavenly mouth." —CHARLES READE ("Peg Woffington").

TO make angel-cake, which was doubtless the kind referred to in the above quotation, beat until very stiff the whites of eleven eggs; add a cupful and a half of granulated sugar and beat again and flavor with a teaspoonful of almond extract. To one cup of sifted flour add a teaspoonful of cream of tartar and sift four times. Mix lightly, with as little beating as possible, into the sugar and eggs. Bake in a cakepan with funnel for forty or forty-five minutes, dusting the pan lightly with flour instead of buttering it. When done invert on glasses or cups till it cools a little.

MAY 6TH

"We have got three things left, Sir—Love, Music and Salad!" —WILKIE COLLINS ("The Moonstone").

A MAYONNAISE properly prepared can be adapted to innumerable uses, and is easily made. Mix with the yolk of an egg half a saltspoonful each of mustard and pepper, a saltspoonful of salt, and the juice of a lemon, stirring lightly. Begin by adding oil, two or three drops at a time, increasing the quantity as the dressing thickens until about three-quarters of a cupful has been used, stirring steadily. Then put in a tablespoonful of vinegar and when that is well blended stir in a quarter of a cupful of oil. Oil, egg, and utensils should be chilled before beginning the mixing.

MAY 7TH

"They are up already and call for eggs and butter."—SHAKESPEARE ("Henry IV.").

THOUGH the good English Shakespeare did not describe the morning eggs as cooked "sur le plat," he may very well have meant to indicate that excellent dish which is prepared by breaking the requisite number of eggs on a plate warmed in the oven, and well buttered, being careful not to let the eggs touch each other. Season each egg with salt and pepper and put a bit of butter on each. A little minced parsley sprinkled over them is an improvement.

MAY 8TH

"A cheap, but wholesome salad from the brook."
—BEAUMONT and FLETCHER.

WATER-CRESS is a very welcome spring salad, too often condemned to appear only as a garnish. It is excellent served with a French dressing, or for breakfast, eaten simply with salt.

MAY 9TH

"I'd give a hundred pounds for a mutton chop."
—CHARLES READE ("It Is Never Too Late To Mend").

THE heavy "English" chops as they are called, are cut from the loin, and should weigh, when trimmed, about a pound each. They should be broiled over an even fire, for about ten minutes, turning often. A piece of the kidney is often broiled and

served with the chop; also a spoonful of
maitre d'hôtel butter, made by beating
into a quarter of a cup of butter a teaspoonful of salt, a saltspoonful of pepper,
and a tablespoonful each of lemon-juice
and chopped parsley.

MAY 10TH

"I'll be with you in the squeezing of a lemon."
GOLDSMITH ("She Stoops to Conquer").

SOAK a package of gelatine in a
cup of cold water until it is all absorbed. Strain the juice of one
orange and three lemons, in which the
grated peel of one lemon has been soaked
for an hour, upon three cupfuls of sugar.
Put into a bowl with the soaked gelatine and pour over all a quart of boiling
water. Stir for a moment or two, then
strain through a bag of cheese-cloth of
double thickness.

MAY 11TH

"'Are there any tea-cakes?' asked the young
mistress."—CHARLOTTE BRONTË ("Shirley").

CREAM a heaping tablespoonful of
butter and a cupful of sugar and
add two well beaten eggs, stirring
briskly for a few moments. Then put

in a cupful of sweet milk. Mix with two cupfuls of sifted flour, three teaspoonfuls of baking-powder and sift again. Stir into the cake mixture, and season with nutmeg and a little of the grated rind of a lemon. Bake in patty-pans and eat before the cakes are cold.

MAY 12TH

"I wish you could ha' seen the shepherd walkin' into the ham and muffins."—CHARLES DICKENS ("Pickwick Papers").

TO serve with muffins, cut thin slices of cold boiled ham, season highly with paprika, mustard, and lemon juice and broil two minutes. Half a glass of currant jelly heated up with a teaspoonful of butter and a little chopped cold ham stirred into it makes an excellent gravy for those who like sweet sauces with meats.

MAY 13TH

"This half of a curd-white smooth cheese-ball."
—ROBERT BROWNING ("The Englishman in Italy").

ADD to a cream cheese half a cupful of chopped walnuts; work them well together, adding, if necessary, a spoonful of cream or milk.

With butter paddles make into balls the size of an English walnut. Pass with the salad.

MAY 14TH

"A despatcher for the preparation of lobster and coffee, and an apparatus for the cooking of toast and mutton chops."—ANTHONY TROLLOPE ("The Warden").

ONE of the simplest and quickest chafing-dish preparations is made by heating in the pan, but not browning, a piece of butter the size of a large egg; when very hot add the meat from two medium-sized or three small lobsters, cut in rather small pieces; toss with a fork while cooking and add a good saltspoonful of salt and a liberal sprinkling of paprika. Serve on very hot plates with hot crackers or toast.

MAY 15TH

"The crême de maraschino led her thoughts back to Italy."—LORD LYTTON ("Parisians").

BOIL two quarts of water with one pound of sugar for fifteen minutes. Take from the fire and when cool add the juice of five large lemons. Freeze, and when about half frozen, add half a pint of maraschino. Cover the freezer and allow the punch to remain packed in ice fully two hours before serving.

MAY 16TH

"Faire was the dawne, and but e'en now the skies
Shew'd like to cream enspir'd with strawberries."
—HERRICK ("Poems").

NO better way for using strawberries has been invented than serving the perfect fruit with sugar and rich cream, being careful that you have sweet berries. When the flavor is good and the size is satisfactory, a pretty way to serve them is with their hulls and stems on, in glass saucers, with a little pyramid of fruit sugar in the centre.

MAY 17TH

"There were fowls, and tongue, and trifle, and sweets, and lobster salad, and potted beef—and everything."—CHARLES DICKENS ("Sketches by Boz").

LARGE lobsters are best for salad, as there is much waste in small ones. Put in boiling water, head downward, and cook for three-quarters of an hour. Carefully break the shells, throw away the stomach, the vein that runs through the tail-piece, and the spongy bits between shell and body. Cut the rest of the meat into small pieces, arrange on lettuce leaves and cover with mayonnaise dressing into which you have stirred the corral and green fat of the lobster.

MAY 18TH

"Have you this spring eaten any 'sparagus yet?"
—BROME.

SCRAPE the stalks of the asparagus, cutting off the tough ends, and place in cold water for half an hour; then cook in hot salted water for half an hour. Put on thin slices of toast on a hot platter and pour over it a white sauce, or simply melted butter.

MAY 19TH

"The tea consumed was the very best, the coffee the very blackest, the cream the very thickest; there was dry toast and buttered toast, muffins and crumpets; hot bread and cold bread, white bread and brown bread, home-made bread and bakers' bread, wheaten bread and oaten bread, and if there be other breads than these they were there."—
ANTHONY TROLLOPE ("The Warden").

BROWN bread delicately toasted with a cream sauce poured over it is delicious. The sauce is made as follows: Into a tablespoonful of butter stir a tablespoonful of flour, add to a pint of boiling cream well seasoned with salt. Just before removing from the fire beat an egg through the sauce and strain through a fine strainer. This last operation is one which the ordinary cook regards as entirely superfluous, but in it lies much of the secret of delicacy in cream sauces.

MAY 20TH

"There was pastry upon a dish; he selected an apricot-puff and a damson tart."—CHARLOTTE BRONTË ("Shirley").

THE ordinary puff-paste patty shells of the confectioner may be bought and made to appear quite an individual dessert by putting in each two or three pieces of canned apricot, sprinkling them rather thickly with granulated sugar and setting them in the oven long enough for the sugar to melt. If the oven is pretty hot it will be well to cover with brown paper. After a few moments take from the oven and strew the top with blanched and chopped almonds—or other nuts. Of course the always admired whipped cream may be added for an extra touch.

MAY 21ST

"But you'd like a drink o' whey first, p'r'aps, I know you're fond o' whey as most folks is when they hanna got to crush it out."—GEORGE ELIOT ("Adam Bede").

"CURDS and whey" have a pastoral sound, but not always an agreeable taste to the uninitiated citizen. The following recipe for white wine whey suggests, however, a warm and welcome drink for a chill autumn day. Put half a pint of fresh milk on the fire; as soon as it boils pour in raisin wine until it is completely turned and looks clear. Boil up again, then set aside until the curd subsides and do not stir it. Pour the whey off, add half a pint of boiling water and a tablespoonful of sugar.

MAY 22D

"It is not the trout one thinks of when one dines with Mrs. Dale."—BULWER ("My Novel").

CLEAN, wash and dry fresh trout; roll in flour, salted and peppered, and fry in deep fat to a delicate golden brown. Serve upon a napkin placed on a hot dish. No sauce can improve the flavor.

MAY 23D

"Wery good thing is weal pie, when you know the lady as made it, and is quite sure it an't kittens." —CHARLES DICKENS ("Pickwick Papers").

A VEAL pie with baked dumplings is an agreeable change, if, as Mr. Weller suggests, you know the lady who makes it. Cut up two pounds of veal in small pieces and stew gently for an hour in a gravy made of a tablespoonful of butter and a tablespoonful of flour, rubbed together, and a quart of water added. At the end of the hour, pour the meat and gravy (which should have been seasoned with salt and pepper) into a shallow baking-dish. Make a biscuit dough and pull off pieces of it with a fork; place these on the dish of meat and bake in a hot oven until brown. Serve immediately.

MAY 24TH

"First we talked about the weather, next about muffins and crumpets. Crumpets, he said he liked best."—THACKERAY ("The Yellowplush Papers").

M IX two pints and a half of sifted flour, a teaspoonful of salt and a half-cup of sugar. Dissolve a quarter of a cake of compressed yeast in two and a half cupfuls of lukewarm water, mix with the flour into a smooth batter and let stand in a warm place over night, covered. In the morning beat half a teacupful of melted butter into the risen batter, fill buttered muffin pans with the mixture, let rise for about an hour, and bake half an hour in a fairly quick oven.

MAY 25TH

"If the cream-cheeses be white, far whiter the hands that made them."—ARTHUR HUGH CLOUGH ("The Bothie of Tober-na-Vuolich").

PLACE upon the range a panful of entirely fresh milk; let it come very slowly to the scalding point, being careful that it does not boil. Put it in a cold place for six hours, then skim off the cream and press gently into little cups, sifting a little salt over the surface of each portion. Set away in a cold place. The result is very delicate cream cheese.

MAY 26TH

"The sauce is costly for it far exceeds the cates."
—GREENE ("Never Too Late").

MAKE a hard sauce by rubbing into half a cup of butter one cup of powdered sugar. Beat or stir till very creamy. Add a quart of sweet ripe strawberries, beating well. It may be made into a liquid sauce by setting the bowl containing it into a pan of hot water and stirring rapidly for a moment or two. This sauce is warranted to turn the plainest cottage pudding into a delightful dessert.

MAY 27TH

"Did I eat any lettuce to supper last night that I am so sleepy?"—J. COAKE.

CUT the roots of the lettuce off even with the head and remove the wilted leaves. Wash carefully. Lay the head in a baking-pan in which has been placed stock enough to cover the pan an inch deep. Cover and place in a moderate oven until the lettuce is soft, which will usually be in about half an hour. Add more stock if necessary. Lift the lettuce out with a fork on to a hot dish. Season the gravy in the pan with salt and pepper and thicken with flour rolled in butter; or the flour may be omitted and it may be thickened with an egg, in which case add butter.

MAY 28TH

"If you give me any conserves give me conserves of beef."—SHAKESPEARE ("Taming of the Shrew").

PUT through a meat grinder, or chop very fine, the tough ends of beefsteak or the unattractive remnants of roast beef. Place in a saucepan with enough gravy or stock to cover it well, or, lacking these, any meat extract; season highly with salt and pepper, a little catsup or Worcestershire sauce, and cook slowly for two or three hours. Pour into a bowl or porcelain dish and when cool set in the ice-box. When cold, slice. Garnish with hard boiled eggs.

"Would he have a cup of coffee, or would he prefer sherbet? Sherbet! . . . He had, however, an idea that sherbet should be drunk sitting cross-legged, and as he was not quite up to this, he ordered the coffee."—ANTHONY TROLLOPE ("The Warden").

UPON four teaspoonfuls of good tea, Ceylon or English Breakfast rather than Oolong, pour one quart of boiling water. Cover it closely and allow it to stand five minutes, then strain and set in a cool place. When the tea is cold put a large piece of ice in the punch-bowl, also a cupful and a half of granulated sugar, and six tablespoonfuls of strained lemon-juice. Add the tea and, just as you serve, a pint of Apollinaris, or carbonated water.

MAY 30TH

"Some arrowroot of a very superior quality was speedily despatched."—JANE AUSTEN ("Emma").

ARROWROOT is not only excellent for gruels and blanc-manges, but the most delicate thickening for soups. A good broth is made by stirring two teaspoonfuls of arrowroot into a little cold water until smooth, then adding it to strong consommé. It improves the flavor and increases the nutritious quality of the soup.

MAY 31ST

"That I may reach that happy time
   The kindly gods I pray,
For are not ducks and peas in prime
   Upon the last of May?"
—THACKERAY ("Poems").

HALF roast a duck; put it into a stew-pan with a pint of beef gravy, a couple of leaves of sage and a leaf of mint cut small, pepper and salt and an onion (minced). Simmer fifteen minutes and skim. Add one quart of green peas. Cover closely and cook half an hour longer. Put in a piece of butter and a couple of table-spoonfuls of flour, boil through and serve in one dish.

JUNE 1ST

"I know where wild strawberries abound."—
CHARLOTTE BRONTË ("Shirley").

STRAWBERRIES are too delicate to brandy acceptably, but an old English way to preserve them is to fill a pint jar with the berries, sifting

through them three heaping tablespoonfuls of granulated sugar and pour in
as much Madeira or sherry as the jar
will hold. The wild strawberries, with
their rich flavor, are particularly good
for this.

JUNE 2D

"After all, Gandrin, when we lose the love-letters,
it is some consolation that *laitances de carpes* and
sautés de foie gras are still left to fill up the void in
our hearts."—LORD LYTTON ("Parisians").

AMERICAN hearts must be con-
soled by the roe of shad instead
of the roe of carp. The most delicious way of cooking this delicacy is
to fry it, but for those who rebel against
fried food the following method may be
recommended. Make a thick brown
sauce by cooking butter and flour together in equal quantities until a rich
brown, then adding a pint of cream or
milk and salt and pepper. Boil the
shad roes ten minutes, then place in a
baking-dish, pour the sauce over them,
and bake for three-quarters of an hour
in a moderate oven. Garnish with parsley and hard boiled egg.

JUNE 3D

"There was a delicate fricassee of sweetbread and some asparagus brought in at first, and good Mr. Woodhouse, not thinking the asparagus quite boiled enough, sent it all away again."—JANE AUSTEN ("Emma").

FOR a delicious fricassee put a teaspoonful of butter into a chafing-dish pan. Fry to a delicate brown three nicely cleaned sweetbreads cut in small pieces. Add half a pint of chicken broth, a teaspoonful of flour, a tablespoonful of finely chopped celery, a dash of cayenne pepper, a teaspoonful of salt, and half a teacupful of asparagus tips previously boiled tender.

JUNE 4TH

"They tempt me, your beans there: spare a plate."—ROBERT BROWNING ("The Bean Feast").

THE stringed beans of what may be called the cooking of commerce are seldom tempting, but the following method of preparing them can be recommended to the most fastidious "bean-feaster." String the beans carefully, slit them lengthwise into thin strips. Salt and cook them until nearly tender, then pour off the water, and replace it with a cupful of white stock or of milk in which a tablespoonful of butter, blended with as much flour, has been stirred. Finish cooking and serve at once.

JUNE 5TH

"My heart sank with our claret-flask."—ROBERT BROWNING.

FOR claret-cup dilute a quart of good claret with a pint of ice-water; add a large cup of granulated sugar, the juice of three lemons and one orange. Half an hour before serving put into it half a dozen long sprigs of fresh mint and a cucumber sliced lengthwise, half a dozen slices of a small orange, the same of lemon, and, if in season, a few strawberries or raspberries, and two or three pieces of sliced pineapple. Serve ice cold. This is an orthodox rule but the cucumber may be omitted with profit for many tastes.

JUNE 6TH

"Hark, the quick whistling pelt of the olives."
—BROWNING ("The Englishmen in Italy").

RIPE olives minced and stirred into scrambled eggs add a delectable flavor to a simple dish. The eggs should be cooked very rare.

JUNE 7TH

"We'll have a dozen of bones well charged with marrow."—CARTWRIGHT.

HAVE the marrow bones cut in lengths of two or three inches, wash and wipe the bones, covering the ends with a stiff dough of flour and water. Fasten the bones in a piece of cloth, put in a sauce-pan with enough boiling water to cover them and boil for an hour; then remove both cloth and dough. They may be served simply as they are, with pieces of buttered toast, or may have the marrow removed and spread on hot toast. A still better way for the marrow lover is to spread it on steak, especially tenderloin, and always very hot.

JUNE 8TH

"Pineapple is great. She is indeed almost too transcendent—a delight, if not sinful, yet so like to sinning, that really a tender conscienced person would do well to pause."—CHARLES LAMB.

TO one pound of sugar add three pints of boiling water and cook for half an hour. Pare a fine pineapple (the yellow ones are best), and grate it, or, better still, tear from the core with a silver fork. Add four table-spoonfuls of lemon-juice and the pulp of an orange. When the boiled syrup is cool, pour into it the pineapple and orange and pack away in ice for two or three hours. When ready to serve pour in a glass of sherry or Madeira and a few strawberries or stoned cherries, if in season. Put into a punch-bowl with a block of ice.

JUNE 9TH

"I quitted the 'Rose Cottage Hotel' with deep regret, believing that I should see nothing so pleas-ant as its gardens and its veal-cutlets and its dear little bowling green, elsewhere."—THACKERAY.

VEAL cutlets fried with a gravy are certainly not a very whole-some dish, despite the fact that they are undeniably appetizing. The following recipe gives perhaps the most delicate way known of preparing this indigestible meat. Cut the slices about three-quarters of an inch thick. Dip them first in egg and then in bread-crumbs seasoned with salt, pepper and chopped parsley. Broil them over a clear fire and serve with butter and catsup.

JUNE 10TH

"And, upon my word, the very thing my soul was longing for—a cup of coffee!"—MRS. HUM-PHRY WARD ("Lady Rose's Daughter").

THE difficulty of getting a good cup of coffee when traveling is sometimes great, and it may be avoided by carrying a bottle of perco-lated coffee in one's outfit. Put one pound of pulverized coffee in a glass chemist's funnel, the smaller end of which has been stopped with absorbent cotton. The coffee must first be mois-tened with a cupful of water stirred thoroughly through it. After putting the coffee in the funnel pour over it one quart and half a pint of cold water. Set the funnel over a jar and let the water percolate through the coffee. The ex-tract obtained will make strong coffee used in the proportion of five teaspoonfuls to a coffee cupful of boiling water. Add the coffee to the water, not the water to the coffee. In a cool place this will keep a fortnight without difficulty.

JUNE 11TH

"When you are tired of eating strawberries in the garden, there shall be cold meat in the house." —JANE AUSTEN ("Emma").

STRAWBERRIES from the garden should be served on their own leaves, dusted with powdered sugar, and each delightful little heap crowned with whipped cream. To preserve them in a way to keep their garden flavor, stew one-quarter of them, squeeze the juice through a bag as for jelly, cook the remainder of the berries in this juice, to which sugar enough to make a rich syrup has been added.

JUNE 12TH

"Greens, oddly bruised, formed the accompanying vegetable."—CHARLOTTE BRONTË ("Shirley").

BEET-TOP greens mixed with dandelion greens are delicious in the Spring of the year. They should be carefully washed and boiled fast for twenty minutes in merely enough water to keep them from burning until their own juices are extracted by the heat. When they are cooked drain them thoroughly in a colander, and add a large lump of butter and a little salt and pepper, but do not chop as in the case of spinach. People with an old-fashioned taste for rich and homely flavors like to boil with them a piece of salt pork, serving it in the same dish.

JUNE 13TH

"O'er our parched tongue the rich metheglin glides,
And the red dainty trout the knife divides."
—GAY.

BRILLAT SAVARIN tells us not to forget that trout should be fried in the finest olive oil, made hot enough to brown a cube of bread in five or six seconds. So cooked he declares it is a dish fit for a cardinal, which in Italy means much more than "fit for a king."

JUNE 14TH

"You've got the basket with the Veal and Ham-Pie and things, and the bottles of Beer?"—CHARLES DICKENS ("Cricket on the Hearth").

THE modern recipes for veal-and-ham pie are not so elaborate and costly as the best of the old English pies—neither are they so good. Here is the original rule: Cut thin slices from the breast of veal; season them with salt and pepper. Slice two sweetbreads and season these also. Lay a puff paste "on the ledge of the dish," and fill the latter with alternate layers of veal sweetbreads, hard-boiled eggs, and oysters, with a layer of thin slices of ham at the top. Truffles and mushrooms are sometimes added. Pour over the mixture a pint of veal stock slightly thickened. Cover with puff paste and bake slowly two hours. Half an hour before serving insert a funnel in the crust and pour in a cup of rich cream.

JUNE 15TH

"Fill all fruit with ripeness to the core."—KEATS.

A VERY good use to make of all fruit which needs to have the quality of "ripeness to the core" is to make Brandy Tutti Frutti. Begin with strawberries; prepare three pounds as for eating; put in a large jar with three pounds of granulated sugar and a quart of brandy and cover tightly. Stir often, and when raspberries are ripe add two or three pounds of them with an equal amount of sugar. Add other fruits as they ripen, always with the same weight of sugar. Peaches should be pared and quartered, and sweet plums should be peeled and cut up; if any very acid fruit be added, cook it first. Stir frequently, keep tightly corked in a cool place, and you will have a delicious and unusual accompaniment for creams and ices.

JUNE 16TH

"Shall it be a delicate lobster-salad? or a dish of elegant tripe and onions?"—THACKERAY.

F OR those who like lobster, and do not like mayonnaise, a salad may be prepared by cutting the good parts of the lobster into rather small pieces and mixing with them the yolks of half a dozen hard-boiled eggs cut in bits; toss together with a silver fork, add a good French dressing of three table-spoonfuls of oil to one of vinegar. Pepper and salt to taste. Arrange on lettuce-leaves with the whites of the eggs and olives as a garnish.

JUNE 17TH

"The whole vegetable tribe have lost their gust with me. Only I stick to asparagus, which still seems to inspire gentle thoughts."—CHARLES LAMB.

PUT half a bunch of asparagus from which the tips have been removed into three pints of stock (or water). Fry an onion and add a bay leaf, a little parsley and a stalk of celery, tied together. Put in the soup with twelve peppercorns and a level teaspoonful of salt, and simmer for thirty-five minutes. Strain through a sieve, pressing through all the asparagus possible. Put the strained soup on the fire; add two tablespoonfuls of flour and two of butter, rubbed together; cook ten minutes; add a cup of cream and the asparagus-tips, which should have cooked twenty minutes in stock or milk. Serve at once.

JUNE 18TH

"Therefor, out with the cold pies, out with the salads, and the chickens, and the champagne."
—THACKERAY.

FOR chicken salad cut the chicken into small pieces, being careful to remove any bits of skin and gristle. Marinade with equal quantities of oil and vinegar, seasoned with salt and pepper. Set in a cool place for a couple of hours; when ready to use mix with the chicken about a third of the quantity of chopped celery, or, if it is not in season, bits of lettuce leaves, torn, not cut, apart. Then stir in about the same quantity of English walnut meats as of celery. Mix with it all a little mayonnaise, and on the top spread more of the mayonnaise. Serve in white lettuce leaves.

JUNE 19TH

"And we must glorify
A mushroom! one of yesterday!"
        —BEN JONSON ("Catiline").

WASH and peel a pint of fresh mushrooms, cook gently for five minutes in enough salted boiling water to just cover them; then add a scant tablespoonful of butter, season with paprika and a gill of red wine, cover and bring the stew to a boil.

JUNE 20TH

"A dish of thick bread and scraped butter, a plate of hard biscuit, a teapot, and a glass milk-jug."
—ANNIE I. THACKERAY ("Out of the World").

HARD biscuit made at home are the joy of dyspeptics and are very simple to make if the cook is not afraid to use the strength of her arm. Rub a piece of butter the size of a large hickory-nut into a pint of sifted flour to which a teaspoonful of salt has been added. Mix with the beaten white of an egg and warm milk into a stiff paste. Beat this with a rolling-pin for half an hour. Then form the dough into small balls, roll out thin, and bake a very light brown.

JUNE 21ST

"Yes, by Saint Anne, and ginger shall be hot i' the mouth, too."—SHAKESPEARE ("Twelfth Night").

THIS ginger shall be hot and cold, too, the poison carrying its own antidote. Make a rich custard of one quart of milk and eight eggs, whites and yolks beaten together; when the eggs are light beat in four cupfuls of sugar and one quart of cream. Scald the milk before adding to sugar and eggs; return the mixture to the fire in a double boiler; stir until the custard thickens; when cool flavor with vanilla and beat in the cream. Put in the freezer and when half frozen stir in a cupful of preserved ginger in bits and two table-spoonfuls of the ginger syrup. Cover the freezer and finish freezing.

JUNE 22D

"But a plain leg of mutton, my dear,
 I beg thee get ready at three;
Have it smoking, and tender and juicy,
 And what better meat can there be?"
—THACKERAY ("Memorials of Gormandising").

THE "plain leg of mutton" may be robbed of some of its plainness by having the bone removed and stuffing it with a mixture of grated bread crumbs, seasoned highly with salt, pepper, and any of the herbs preferred— thyme, sage, or marjoram, and a liberal allowance of melted butter, say a third of a cup. If a moist stuffing is liked, add a little hot stock, but using only butter makes it better for most people. Garnish with parsley.

JUNE 23D

"Come and eat my strawberries; they are ripening fast."—JANE AUSTEN ("Emma").

IF there exist any who are tired of eating or serving strawberries plain, we have the authority of Savarin and the Count de la Plàce for dressing them with orange juice just before they are to be eaten.

JUNE 24TH

"When the ducks and green peas came, we looked at each other in dismay."—MRS. GASKELL ("Cranford").

PEOPLE who like to combine two spring flavors which seem to have little enough in common, add to green peas while they are cooking a few leaves of fresh mint, chopped. An old recipe suggests also adding a head of lettuce and a sliced onion, but to the modern taste this seems very much like painting the lily.

JUNE 25TH

"The foolish John
Resolved the problem, 'twixt his napkined thumbs,
Of what was signified by taking soup
Or choosing mackerel."
—MRS. BROWNING ("Aurora Leigh").

SELECT a fat salt mackerel weighing at least a pound; soak over night, in a pan of cold water, skin side up so that the salt falls out; change the water in the morning. Drain well and put on the fire in cold water; when it boils drain thoroughly and gently remove the backbone. Pour over and in the mackerel two tablespoonfuls of nicely browned melted butter. Garnish with parsley and serve very hot.

JUNE 26TH

"'Wot's the matter?' says the doctor.
"'Wery ill,' says the patient.
"'Wot have you been eatin' on?' says the doctor.
"'Roast weal,' says the patient."—CHARLES DICKENS ("Pickwick Papers").

UNDOUBTEDLY there are people to whom indulgence in roast veal means a doctor's bill; but they are comparatively few. If veal is thoroughly cooked it may generally be eaten with impunity. Have the bone taken out of a fillet. Stuff with bread-crumbs highly seasoned and bound lightly together with butter; no other moistening is needed. Skewer the meat into shape, cover it with slices of salt pork or bacon. Cook at least three hours, whether the fillet is large or small. That length of time is needed to make the stubborn fibre of the meat digestible.

JUNE 27TH

"Reserve the feast ! The board forsake—
   Ne'er tap the wine—don't cut the cake—
  No toasts or foolish speeches make
   At which my reason spurns."
                —HOOD ("Poems").

DELICIOUS old fashioned "delicate" cake is made by creaming together one cupful of butter with two of sugar, then slowly adding one cupful of sweet milk and the whites of eight eggs, beaten to a stiff froth. Finally mix in, with as little stirring as possible, three cupfuls of sifted flour in which has been stirred three teaspoonfuls of baking-powder. Flavor with one teaspoonful of almond extract. The addition at the last of a cupful of blanched and chopped almonds, with an icing which is ornamented with rings of whole blanched almonds, transforms this into a christening cake of the most orthodox type.

JUNE 28TH

"Mine eyes smell onions, I shall weep anon."
—SHAKESPEARE ("All's Well That Ends Well").

SPANISH onion is eaten as a salad without cooking, mixing it with the white, inner leaves of lettuce. Peel the onion, and, not to let the "eyes smell" it too weepingly, do it under water. Shred the onion fine. Put the lettuce leaves and onion shavings in a bowl, cover with a French dressing of six tablespoonfuls of oil, three of vinegar, half a teaspoonful of salt, and a pinch of pepper. The young, small garden onions in the early Spring are often eaten raw with a simple dressing, and also mixed with cucumbers and radishes.

JUNE 29TH

"What's the Latin name for parsley?"—BROWNING ("Soliloquy of the Spanish Cloister").

PARSLEY butter is very nice for fish, flesh, or fowl, and still nicer for boiled potatoes. Add to half a cup of butter a tablespoonful of lemon-juice, one of chopped parsley, half a teaspoonful of salt and the same amount of paprika. Beat thoroughly, and if it is to be used for fish stir in a teaspoonful of capers.

JUNE 30TH

"There is such a beautiful piece of cold beef in the larder; do somebody ask for a little slice of it."
—THACKERAY ("Memorials of Gormandizing").

IN roasting beef that is not to be eaten until it is cold especial care needs to be taken to keep the juices in. If a rib roast is chosen, have the ribs removed and the meat rolled and securely tied with twine, a couple of skewers fastening the end. Put in a very hot oven for ten minutes to sear the surface, or, if that is not practicable, pour a little boiling water over it, dredge with flour and set in an oven where it will cook fast for fifteen minutes. Cool your oven, or remove to one not so hot; allow ten minutes to a pound; baste often, and when done season with salt and pepper and butter. Let it get entirely cold before putting on the ice.

"The dinner was as well-dressed as any I ever saw. The venison was roasted to a turn—and everybody said they never saw so fat a haunch. The soup was fifty times better than what we had at the Lucases' last week; and even Mr. Darcy acknowledged that the partridges were uncommonly well done."—JANE AUSTEN ("Pride and Prejudice").

SORREL soup has a peculiarly appetizing sound and its flavor corresponds. In the country it may be made by cooking the sorrel as you would spinach until it is tender and adding it to white stock slightly thickened and seasoned with salt and very little white pepper. In large cities it is now possible to get a bottled sorrel purée prepared in France which is almost as good as the fresh sorrel to use for soups and sauces.

JULY 2D

"That last cherry soothes a roughness of my palate."—ROBERT BROWNING ("Fust and His Friends").

STONE three pounds of cherries; put them in a preserving kettle with two pounds of granulated sugar mixed through them; simmer till they begin to shrivel; then strain them from the juice; dry them in a cool oven, being careful not to have them cook more. Spread them out on plates to finish drying.

JULY 3D

"Beamish got the flowers. . . . I only stood the cakes. Now, then, Catharine you must make tea, please."—ANNIE THACKERAY ("The Village on the Cliff").

TO make very rich jumbles that will keep indefinitely (unless eaten) take a large cup of butter, two heaping cups of powdered sugar, four eggs, the juice and rind of two lemons, half a nutmeg, a small half teaspoonful of soda, with just milk enough to dissolve it, and flour to make it as soft a dough as will roll out. Roll very thin until the dough is nearly transparent, sprinkle with granulated sugar, cut out with a cookie cutter and bake in a quick oven.

JULY 4TH

"Next came a great piece of salmon, likewise on a silver dish."—THACKERAY ("The History of Samuel Titmarsh").

SEW the fish into a coarse cloth or mosquito netting and boil twelve minutes to the pound in salted water, to which the juice of a couple of lemons has been added. Serve with Hollandaise sauce.

Rule for sauce: Beat half a cup of butter creamy, add the yolks of four raw eggs and blend with the butter. Then add a tablespoonful and a half of lemon-juice, half a teaspoonful of salt, and a pinch of cayenne pepper. Place the bowl in a pan of boiling water, add a third of a cupful of boiling water to the mixture and cook until it thickens, beating it continually.

JULY 5TH

"Found the fowl duly brown, both back and breast."—ROBERT BROWNING ("The Ring and the Book").

MARYLAND fried chicken has a fame dating back long "befo' de wah." The old mammies fry thin slices of bacon in the pan, then turn their young chickens, cut up as for fricassee, salted and peppered and rolled in flour, into the hot fat. Fry till each piece is a beautiful brown. Take the chicken and bacon out of the pan and put them in the oven to keep hot. Stir into the gravy a tablespoonful of flour, and when it browns add a pint of rich cream. Serve with hot soda biscuits.

JULY 6TH

"Jars of pickles and preserves, and cheeses and boiled hams, and rounds of beef, arranged on the shelves in the most tempting and delicious array."
—CHARLES DICKENS ("Pickwick Papers").

FILL glass jars with large cherries, stemmed but not stoned. Boil together for ten minutes a pint of vinegar, four tablespoonfuls of white sugar, twelve whole cloves, twelve whole allspice, six blades of mace and some stick cinnamon. Allow the vinegar to cool, strain and pour over the cherries, sealing the jars. This will be about the right quantity of vinegar for two quarts of cherries.

JULY 7TH

"After this a stewed pigeon, faced by greengage tart, and some yellow cream twenty-four hours old; item, an iced pudding."—CHARLES READE ("It Is Never Too Late To Mend").

WHIP a pint and a half of rich cream, sweeten with half a cupful of powdered sugar and add half a pint of crushed ripe raspberries. Beat well, put into a mould and pack with ice and rock salt, and allow to stand for three hours.

JULY 8TH

"One of those young women who almost invariably, though one hardly knows why, recall to one's mind the idea of a cold fillet of veal."—CHARLES DICKENS ("Sketches by Boz").

ONE of the best ways to remove the objectionable features from cold veal is to slice it as thin as possible with a sharp knife; marinade with a dressing of two tablespoonfuls each of oil and vinegar, a saltspoonful of salt and half as much pepper. Let it stand in the dressing two hours, then pile lightly on lettuce leaves, cover with mayonnaise and garnish with hard boiled eggs cut in lengthwise quarters.

JULY 9TH

"Bless my soul! our words used to come out like brandy-cherries; but now a sentence is like raspberry jam, on the stage and off."—CHARLES READE ("Peg Woffington").

TO brandy cherries pack glass jars with the fruit (white cherries are best for this purpose); to each jar allow four heaping tablespoonfuls of granulated sugar, putting a layer of cherries, then sugar, and so on till the jars are full. Then pour in brandy till no more can be put in. Fasten down the tops, put the jars in a dark place, and after a few weeks the cherries will be ready to use.

JULY 10TH

"I was just in the act of despatching the last morsel of the most savoury stewed lamb and rice, which had formed my meal."—THACKERAY ("The Tremendous Adventures of Major Gahagan").

CUT a pound of meat from the breast of lamb. Put into a frying-pan with an onion which has been minced and fried brown in hot butter. Cook for a few moments over a hot fire until the meat has browned slightly. Then add a teaspoonful of paprika and a tablespoonful of flour and cook five minutes longer before adding two cupfuls of hot lamb broth. Season with salt to taste and the juice of one lemon and stew very slowly until the lamb is tender. Serve with boiled rice.

JULY 11TH

"The soup was a sort of purée of dried peas, which Mademoiselle had prepared amidst bitter lamentations that in this desolate country of England no haricot beans were to be had."—CHARLOTTE BRONTË ("Shirley").

THE beans of Mademoiselle's lamentation were not the "haricot vert" of which modern visitors to Paris hear and see so much, but lima, or, possibly, kidney beans. The simplest way has never been improved upon, and they are best cooked in boiling water for about half an hour, then drained dry, put in the serving dish, which should be hot, seasoned with salt and pepper, and a spoonful of butter stirred quickly through them.

JULY 12TH

"They were such trouts as, when once tasted, remain forever in the recollection of the commonly grateful mind—rich, flaky, or creamy, full of flavour."—THACKERAY ("The Irish Sketch-Book").

CLEAN the fish, wash it, and dry it carefully. Salt and pepper it and roll it in flour. Butter an oyster broiler and lay the fish, without having been split, upon it. Broil over clear coals. Serve on a hot platter with butter and parsley.

JULY 13TH

"It was near half an hour before we could get her to finish a pint of raspberry between us."— GOLDSMITH ("The Good-Natured Man").

PUT fine dry raspberries into a stone jar, and the jar into a kettle of water till the juice runs ; strain and to every pint add half a pound of sugar, let it boil up once and skim it. When cold put equal quantities of juice and brandy in bottles, shake well and seal.

JULY 14TH

"Sending a plate of muffins across the table at poor me."—THACKERAY.

THACKERAY would not have pitied himself had the muffins been the little huckleberry ones beloved of men and children. Into a quart of flour sift two teaspoonfuls of baking powder and one of salt. Beat three eggs, yolks and whites separately, and into the yolks stir three cups of milk, a tablespoonful of melted butter and a pint of huckleberries, well dredged with an additional cup of flour. Beat for two or three minutes, add the whites of the eggs and bake in patty pans.

JULY 15TH

"I protest I do honor a chine of beef, I do reverence a loin of veal."—BEAUMONT and FLETCHER ("Woman Hater").

A LOIN of veal is a dish worthy of reverence, and if properly cooked it is suited to ordinary digestions, despite its bad name. Remove the bone from the meat; season the latter highly with salt and pepper, and skewer into shape. Cover with sheets of buttered white paper tied around it. Fry a few slices of pork, a sliced onion, and three tablespoonfuls of flour until brown. Add three pints of water and a cup of stewed tomatoes. Place the veal in a roasting-pan, pour the gravy around it, and cook in a slow oven three hours and a half. It will be both tender and savory. Remove the sheets of paper after the first hour.

JULY 16TH

"'Very well,' I cried, 'that's a good girl. I find you are perfectly qualified for making converts, and so go and help your mother to make the gooseberry-pie.'"—GOLDSMITH ("Vicar of Wakefield").

GOOSEBERRIES make a very good tart, especially if combined with currant juice. Choose berries that are not over-ripe, put in a pre-

serving kettle with half a pint of currant juice to each pound of berries.
When they begin to boil, crush them with
a spoon and add sugar in the proportion
of three-quarters of a pound to a pound
of fruit. Simmer slowly for five or
six hours. Fill pie-crust shells and put
a lattice of crust over the top.

JULY 17TH

"When he actually refused currant and raspberry tart—the good Hannah was alarmed."—
THACKERAY ("The Newcomes").

LINE a pie-dish with paste, wash it
over with white of egg and fill with
currants and raspberries, carefully
picked over. Sweeten lavishly and cover
with strips of the pastry crossed in a
lattice pattern. Bake half an hour in
a good oven.

JULY 18TH

"The odor of that spicy cake came back upon
my recollection."—CHARLES LAMB ("Essays of
Elia").

FOR a spice cake beat together one
egg, two-thirds of a cupful each
of molasses, sugar, and butter, one
cupful of milk, two cupfuls and a half
of flour, into which has been sifted two

teaspoonfuls of baking powder; one tablespoonful of mixed spice, and one
tablespoonful of lemon juice and a little
of the grated rind. Bake in a moderate
oven.

JULY 19TH

"They had seldom seen him eat so heartily at any
table but his own; and never before known him
so little disconcerted by the melted butter's being
oiled."—JANE AUSTEN ("Northanger Abbey").

TO melt butter without having it
oil needs only a little care. Mix
one teaspoonful of flour with a
quarter of a pound of good butter. Put
it into a small saucepan with two or
three tablespoonfuls of hot water, shaking it all the time. Milk used instead of
water makes a whiter sauce and is a
little richer.

JULY 20TH

"A clear soup, a bit of fish, a couple of little en-
trées and a nice little roast. That's my kind of a
dinner."—THACKERAY ("Diary of C. James de la
Pluche, Esq.").

A DELICIOUS entrée for a dinner
is made from calf's liver boiled until tender, cut into bits, and rather
highly seasoned with salt, paprika, a little Worcestershire sauce, and just a hint

of mushroom catsup. Mix the seasoning thoroughly through the liver, heat it, and when ready to serve moisten with a little sherry or good Madeira. This may be served in paper shells, ramakins, or puff paste shells.

JULY 21ST

"Cowcumbers are cold in the third degree."— SWIFT.

USE only fresh cucumbers which have had no chance to wilt in the sun. Pare off not only the green outside but most of the tough white about the seeds. Slice thin and allow to stand in iced water for a half hour before eating. Serve with cracked ice in the dish, passing French dressing with the cucumbers. Some people like a little shredded chives with the cucumbers, and the appearance of the dish is thereby improved.

JULY 22D

"She praised the cook this time, declared the fricassee was excellent, and that there were no eels anywhere like those of the Castlewood moats."
—THACKERAY ("Virginians").

SKIN and clean the eel, removing all the fat; cut in short lengths, leave in olive oil and vinegar for half an hour, salt and pepper; roll in egg and cracker dust, and fry in deep fat.

JULY 23D

"A little Stilton cheese brought up the rear with a nice salad. This made way for a foolish trifling dessert of muscatel grapes, guava jelly, and divers kickshaws diluted with agreeable wines."—CHARLES READE ("It Is Never Too Late To Mend").

A "CALEDONIAN trifle" may sound foolish, but it tastes good. Its ingredients are: Eight eggs, a quart of milk, a teacupful of sugar, a teaspoonful of almond extract, a saltspoonful of salt, and half a tumbler of raspberry jam. Reserve the whites of three eggs and the raspberry jam and make a boiled custard of the other ingredients. Beat the whites of three eggs into a stiff froth for the top of the custard and dot with the jam.

JULY 24TH

"Uninebriate liquors, pressed from cooling fruits, sweetened with honey, and deliciously iced."—BULWER ("My Novel").

FOR a fine fruit punch, mix one cupful of lemon juice, two cupfuls of fruit juice, strawberry, raspberry, or cherry (or a combination of the three), with one cupful of grated pineapple, two quarts of water, one cupful of sugar, and three-quarters of a cupful of strained honey. Serve ice-cold. A cupful of sugar may be substituted for the honey.

JULY 25TH

"A nice tongue, not too green nor too salt, and a small saddle of six-tooth mutton, home-bred, home-fed."—CHARLES READE ("It Is Never Too Late To Mend").

TONGUE should be soaked several hours before cooking—over night is usually best. Place it in a kettle with cold water, letting it come slowly to the boiling point and simmer for three or four hours, until it is very tender. Test by piercing with a fork. Let it cool in the liquor in which it was boiled; skin carefully, beginning at the tip.

JULY 26TH

"Even cream, sugar, tea, toast . . . and eggs, even they have their moral." — CHARLES DICKENS ("Martin Chuzzlewit").

TO make rum omelette, break six eggs into a bowl, add three table-spoonfuls of milk and a little salt; beat until light. Turn into a hot frying pan in which a piece of butter has been melted, and shake the pan until the eggs begin to set. Fold over while the inside is still very creamy and serve. At the table pour over the omelette three or four tablespoonfuls of rum, sprinkle well with sugar, and light the liquor that runs down into the plate, basting the omelette with it until the flame is extinguished.

JULY 27TH

"Aslaug on her knees
Knelt by the brightening fire and dropped
The meal into the pot."
—WILLIAM MORRIS ("The Earthly Paradise").

ASLAUG could not have pro-vided a better dish than the simple corn meal mush made by "wetting up" corn meal in cold water until there are no lumps, then stirring it gradually into salted boiling water until—an old recipe dictates—it is so thick the " stick " will stand in it. The stick is the wooden paddle which is now sold at every house-furnishing store, and used to be made from a broomstick handle. The mush should boil slowly two hours. When cold fry in slices half an inch thick first dipped in egg.

JULY 28TH

"Three days out of the seven, indeed, both man and master dined on nothing else but the vegetables in the garden, and the fishes in the neighboring rill."
—BULWER ("My Novel").

AN excellent salad dressing for cold garden vegetables is made thus: Stir together a tablespoonful each of salt, oil, and sugar. Add a tablespoonful of mustard and three raw eggs. When well mixed add slowly a cup of vinegar and lastly a cup of milk. Put in a double boiler and stir until the mixture is as thick as custard. Cool and place on ice. The vinegar will not curdle the milk if this order of mixing the ingredients is followed. The dressing will keep for two or three weeks in a refrigerator.

"Thanks to his clasp-knife, he was able to appropriate a wing of fowl and a slice of ham; a cantlet of cold custard-pudding he thought would harmonize with these articles."—CHARLOTTE BRONTË ("Shirley").

A DELICIOUS custard pudding may be made from this well tried recipe: Beat five eggs and add to them five tablespoonfuls of sugar and the grated rind of an orange, a pint and a half of rich milk and half a teaspoonful of salt. Mix well and pour into small tin moulds, buttered and sugared before they are filled. Set the puddings in a pan of warm water and place in a moderate oven. Bake three-quarters of an hour, or until they are firm in the centre. Serve with a sauce made of two well beaten eggs, half a teaspoonful of flour, a teaspoonful of corn-starch and two of sugar. Mix these ingredients lightly together and beat into them a cup and a half of boiling milk. Stir over the fire until the thickness of rich cream, then add a gill of sherry. Stir again for a couple of minutes and pour over the custards.

JULY 30TH

"What say you to a piece of beef and mustard?
A dish that I do love."—SHAKESPEARE ("Taming
of the Shrew").

PLAIN boiled beef can occasionally
be substituted with profit for the
usual roast or steak, and it is made
very acceptable by serving with it a good
mustard sauce, made by adding to one
teacupful of boiling stock a tablespoonful
of butter rubbed into a teaspoonful of
flour, a tablespoonful of French mustard,
a teaspoonful of dry English mustard, a
tablespoonful of vinegar, a teaspoonful
of sugar, half a teaspoonful of salt, and
a dash or two of paprika.

JULY 31ST

"That good fellow washed the greens, and peeled
the turnips, and broke the plates, and upset iron
pots full of cold water on the fire and made himself
useful in all sorts of ways."—CHARLES DICKENS
("Cricket on the Hearth").

THE Swiss chard makes a delicious summer green, with a more
piquant flavor than spinach.
Wash carefully, throw into a saucepan
with the water still clinging to the leaves;
let it cook slowly till the juices are

drawn out, then let it boil until tender. Drain in a colander, chop fine. Return to the fire and season. To half a peck add a large tablespoonful of butter, half a teaspoonful of salt, and a dash of pepper. Two tablespoonfuls of cream may be used in place of the butter.

AUGUST 1ST

"Requesting a supply of a puree à la bisque aux écrivisse, the clumsy attendant who served him let fall the assiette of vermeille ciselé."—THACKERAY.

PURÉE *à la bisque aux écrivisse*, or, in plain English, crab soup, is made by melting in a saucepan one tablespoonful of butter; when hot add two small onions, minced, and one sweet green pepper, cut up, with the seeds left out; one large tomato, peeled and sliced thin; season with salt and paprika. Add the meat of four boiled crabs with a very little water and stew ten minutes. Heat three cupfuls of rich milk in a separate vessel. Thicken with one tablespoonful of flour, rubbed in two of butter; add a bit of soda, season with salt and paprika; take from the fire and stir with the crab meat. Pour over croutons and serve.

AUGUST 2D

"The bones of a green frog too, wondrous precious."—MIDDLETON ("The Witch").

WASH frogs' legs in cold salted water, drain and scald, then let them simmer an hour in boiled milk. Remove from the milk when cool, take the flesh off the bones, and cut it into small pieces. Make a rich cream sauce; add the frog meat, seasoned with salt and red pepper, and a little lemon juice. Fill patty shells with the mixture and cook in a hot oven ten minutes.

AUGUST 3D

"And hence this halo lives about
The waiter's hands, that reach
To each his perfect pint of stout,
His proper chop to each."
—TENNYSON ("Will Waterproof").

THE chops from the leg, properly "cutlets," the best served breaded, and are prepared by trimming the cutlets, seasoning with salt and pepper, dipping in bread crumbs, then in beaten egg, again in bread crumbs, and frying them in smoking hot fat. If the chops are to be well done, ten minutes will be about the right time for frying, four to six if rare. Tomato sauce is a desirable addition, but not a necessity.

AUGUST 4TH

"The dear, dear muffins of home!"—THACKERAY ("The Adventures of Philip").

MIX a quart of sifted flour with a quart of milk (warmed), in which half a cupful of butter has been melted; half a yeast cake, dissolved in a little warm water, and three well beaten eggs. Set to rise. When light bake in muffin tins in a quick oven.

AUGUST 5TH

"The Moor leans on his cushion
With the pipe between his lips,
And still at frequent intervals
The sweet sherbet he sips."—HOOD.

ANY fruit juice makes good sherbet, but the juice of blackberries (Emerson's "Ethiops sweet") is particularly delicious, especially if the wild fruit can be obtained. Crush three quarts of the berries with a pint of sugar and let them stand for a couple of hours. Add a quart of water and the juice of half a dozen lemons. Boil for twenty minutes, then strain, and after it is cool, freeze in an old-fashioned freezer, beating it well before packing.

AUGUST 6TH

"Please not a seed-cake, but a plum-cake."—THACKERAY.

LITTLE "plum-cakes" m u c h prized in New England, which go by the name of "Hermits," are made by creaming together half a cup of butter and one of sugar; then adding a tablespoonful of milk and two lightly beaten eggs. When these are well mixed add two cups of flour into which has been stirred a heaping teaspoonful of baking powder and a cupful of stoned and chopped raisins. Roll about a quarter of an inch thick, using a little flour to keep from sticking. Cut in rounds and bake ten to fifteen minutes.

AUGUST 7TH

"Banish, dear Mrs. Cook, I beseech you, the whole onion tribe."—CHARLES LAMB ("Essays of Elia").

PROBABLY escalloped o n i o n s were not in Lamb's mind when he uttered his wholesale condemnation, for they are much the least offensive to a sensitive nose. Boil the onions in three quarts of water for an hour, changing the water once. When tender, drain off the water and cut into small pieces; put in a shallow baking dish and pour over them a cream sauce; sprinkle with a cupful of bread crumbs, a tablespoonful of butter or grated rich cheese.

AUGUST 8TH

"A previously hearty sirloin of beef looked as if it had been suddenly seized with the palsy."— CHARLES DICKENS ("Sketches by Boz").

WHEN the sirloin has been reduced to this condition it is not attractive on the table, and if it has fortunately been cooked decidedly rare it can be served as a "dry devil" very acceptably. Make a paste of three tablespoonfuls of oil, two of dry mustard, a teaspoonful of salt, half a teaspoonful of black pepper, and rather less of paprika. Spread the paste over the slices of rare beef and dredge liberally with flour. Have a very hot frying pan, put in it three tablespoonfuls of butter, as needed, cook quickly, and serve as soon as done on a hot dish. If a still hotter dish is desired, increase the mustard and add cayenne.

AUGUST 9TH

"Bestrew'd with lettuce and cool salad herbs."—
BEAUMONT and FLETCHER ("Woman Hater").

THERE are very few vegetables that do not make an excellent addition to a macedoine salad— the "cool salad herbs" are almost unlimited. A few boiled potatoes, a plateful of lima or string beans, of peas, carrots, spinach, or boiled onion, may be harmoniously joined with uncooked celery, cress, or lettuce, and may be blended with a mayonnaise dressing and garnished with olives or capers or sliced cucumber pickle, or may be served with a simple French dressing poured over them.

AUGUST 10TH

"The coffee was boiling over a charcoal fire, and large slices of bread and butter were piled one upon the other like deals in a lumber yard."—CHARLES DICKENS ("Sketches by Boz").

MUCH as French and Vienna coffee have grown in popular favor, some occasions and some people demand the old-fashioned sort, which may be made clear and delicious. Put in a bowl one heaping tablespoonful of ground coffee for each person and one for the pot; add to it sufficient water to moisten it thoroughly; put into the pot with as many cupfuls of boiling water as you have tablespoonfuls of coffee, less one. Add the crushed shell of an egg, or a little of the egg itself, beaten up with water, and allow it to come slowly to the boiling; let it boil two or three minutes; take from the fire, put in a cup of cold water to settle it; put it back on the fire; let it stand for a few minutes and pour into the serving pot, which should be hot.

AUGUST 11TH

"There was a ripe melon, a fish from the river in a memorable Béarnaise sauce, a fat fowl in a fricassee and a dish of asparagus followed by a dish of fruit."—ROBERT LOUIS STEVENSON ("The Treasure of Frauchard").

A PRESENT fashion for serving the small cantaloupes, or muskmelons, is thoroughly to chill the melons on ice; just before serving cut in halves and remove the seeds, putting in each half melon a large spoonful of ice cream, and for this purpose a rather plain cream is preferred. For those whose digestions warrant it this is an agreeable way of combining two favorite dishes.

AUGUST 12TH

"In reply to her sarcastic inquiry, he artlessly owned that he should like another cheese-cake."—THACKERAY ("The Virginians").

MIX the curd of three quarts of milk, a pound of currants, twelve ounces of sugar, a quarter of an ounce of cinnamon, the same of nutmeg, the peel of one lemon, chopped to a paste, the yolks of eight and whites of six eggs, a pint of scalded cream and a glass of brandy. Put a light thin puff-paste in patty pans and three quarters fill them.

AUGUST 13TH

"There's a pillau, Joseph, just as you like it, and papa has brought the best turbot in Billingsgate."—THACKERAY ("Vanity Fair").

FOR a Turkish pillau boil a fowl as for fricassee; add to the water in which it is boiled a teacupful of rice, half a teacupful of raisins, the same amount of blanched almonds, and a red pepper pod, from which the seeds have been carefully removed. Serve with the chicken. It will be a very hot dish.

AUGUST 14TH

"He relieved the bag of a bottle of wine, slices of meat, hard eggs, and lettuce, a chipped cup to fling away after drinking the wine." — GEORGE MEREDITH ("The Amazing Marriage").

AN excellent variation on the hard-boiled eggs of picnics or luncheon baskets is to make them into salad eggs. Remove the shells, cut in halves, take out the yolks, and with a silver fork rub them smooth; stir in oil and vinegar in the proportion of one spoonful of vinegar to two of oil; season with salt and paprika. Replace in the whites and press together. They are very appetizing on a journey.

AUGUST 15TH

"And lo! two puddings smoked upon the board." —POPE.

A SMOKING corn-pudding is a pleasant sight when the mercury is low in summer. Scrape a dozen ears of full-grown corn by slitting each row of kernels with a sharp knife, and then with the back of the knife scraping all the soft part out, leaving the empty hull on the cob. Add a pint of milk, a cup of sugar, a teaspoonful of salt and a tablespoonful of melted butter. Bake three hours in a moderate oven. This dish may be prepared in winter from canned corn, and makes an excellent variety in vegetables to serve with meat if the sugar is left out.

AUGUST 16TH

"Have you sent to the apothecary for a sufficient quantity of cream of tartar to make lemonade?"— COLEMAN ("Man and Wife").

IF we want lemonade as nearly perfect as possible, we use freshly boiled water. This rule has borne the test of repeated trial: For a quart of lemonade take the juice of four lemons and the rind of one, carefully peeled off to get just the yellow outside part. This, cut into pieces, is added to the juice and put in a covered jug or jar with three ounces of sugar. Pour on a quart of water brought to the boiling point as for tea. Let it stand until cold, and turn into a pitcher in which are thin orange slices and bits of pineapple.

AUGUST 17TH

"Deeming that the sight of pickled salmon might work a softening change."—CHARLES DICKENS ("Martin Chuzzlewit").

ANY salmon left over may be converted into this popular dish. Free the fish from skin and bone. Make a sauce by bringing to the boiling point half a cupful of vinegar, two tablespoonfuls of lemon juice, three cloves, a piece of stick cinnamon, a teaspoonful of salt, and a pinch of paprika. As soon as it boils pour it over the cold salmon and set away to cool. It will keep a week or more.

AUGUST 18TH

"That girl, sir, makes the best veal-and-ham pie in England, and I think I can promise ye a glass of punch of the right flavor."—THACKERAY ("Pendennis").

FOR plain veal-and-ham pie cut two pounds of lean veal into small pieces, cover with cold water, add a cupful of boiled ham, chopped very fine, two onions, minced; pepper and salt to taste; stew slowly for two hours. At the end of that time thicken the gravy with two tablespoonfuls of flour, blended

with a tablespoonful of butter. Pour
into a deep baking dish and cover with
a crust of biscuit dough, rolled thin.
Bake twenty minutes in a hot oven.

AUGUST 19TH

"How my cheeks grew red as tomatoes."—ROB-
ERT BROWNING ("A Likeness").

CUT large, fair tomatoes in rather
thick slices; do not peel, as the
skin is needed to preserve the shape
of the slices. Season with salt and pepper, dip in beaten eggs and cracker
crumbs and fry in butter, turning till
brown on both sides. Lift carefully on
to a hot platter, stir into the pan a
scant tablespoonful of browned flour and
three or four chopped olives. Pour over
the tomatoes and serve.

AUGUST 20TH

"And one day my wife spied him with his mouth
smeared all over with our jam-pudding."—THACK-
ERAY ("Contributions to Punch").

SPREAD slices of bread from which
the crusts have been cut, with plenty
of butter and jam. Put them in a
buttered pudding dish and cover with a

custard, made of a quart of scalded milk, five eggs, and a teacupful of sugar. When the bread has soaked up the custard put in another layer and repeat the process until the dish is full. Bake half an hour in a slow oven. Eat with lemon sauce.

AUGUST 21ST

"Treat here, ye shepherds blithe! your damsels sweet,
For pies and cheese-cakes are for damsels meet."
—GAY.

BUTTER a deep plate and cover with a plain pie crust dough; put into it a mixture made by beating together a cupful of cottage (or pot) cheese and stirring into it two tablespoonfuls of sugar beaten up with the yolks of four eggs; add a cupful of dried currants and half a cupful of blanched and chopped almonds, and, finally, the whipped whites of the eggs. Bake in a moderate oven for twenty-five to thirty minutes.

AUGUST 22D

"Like a forked radish, with a head fantastically carved upon it."—SHAKESPEARE ("Henry IV.").

THE white leaves of chicory mixed with thin slices of young radishes and ornamented with the whole radishes as "fantastically carved" as you may choose, make a delicious midsummer salad, dressed either with a French dressing or mayonnaise.

AUGUST 23D

"'Vell,' said Sam, 'this is comin' it rayther powerful, this is. I never heard a biled leg o' mutton called a swarry afore. I wonder wot they'd call a roast one.'"—CHARLES DICKENS ("Pickwick Papers").

REMOVE the fat from the leg of mutton to be boiled, and put it into fast boiling water. After fifteen minutes move to a place on the range where it will only simmer. Allow twelve minutes for each pound if you wish it cooked rare, fifteen minutes if well done. Serve with a white or butter sauce, to which half a cup of capers has been added, or, a very good substitute, an equal quantity of chopped gherkins.

Soup, fish,—shall I have three sorts of fish? I will; they are cheap in this market."—CHARLES READE ("Peg Woffington").

THE cheap perch may be made into a tempting dish for luncheon or dinner when stewed and served with an oyster sauce. Put half a dozen perch into a kettle with half a pint of boiling water, in which has been dissolved a teaspoonful of salt. Cook five minutes. To make the sauce, heat twenty-five oysters in their liquor. When they begin to boil take out the oysters and skim the liquor. Add to it a cupful of sweet milk and cream, and when it boils add a tablespoonful of butter and flour rubbed together. Season with salt and pepper; add the oysters, let it boil up once. Pour the sauce in a dish and add the fish.

AUGUST 25TH

"An exquisite and poignant sauce, for which I'll say unto my cook, 'There's gold, go forth and be a knight.'"—BEN JONSON ("The Alchemist").

BÉARNAISE sauce is the most delicate of poignant sauces to eat with fish or to serve with any kind of meat or fish croquettes. It is made of the yolks of four eggs, four table-spoonfuls of butter, half a teaspoonful of vinegar, a dash of cayenne pepper, three teaspoonfuls of lemon juice and one of tarragon vinegar, one teaspoonful of onion juice, one of chopped parsley and one of capers. Stir the butter in a hot cup until creamy; add the beaten yolks of the eggs. Then add all the other ingredients, except the parsley and capers, and beat again. Cook over boiling water for three minutes, stirring constantly; add the parsley and capers, and serve at once.

AUGUST 26TH

"Miss Barker, in her former sphere, had, I dare say, been made acquainted with the beverage they call cherry-brandy."—MRS. GASKELL ("Cranford").

THE wild cherries are used for the cherry brandy or "cherry bounce" so familiar to readers of English novels. Wash the cherries; crush them slightly, and allow five table-spoonfuls of sugar to each quart jar; when the cherries and sugar are well mixed in the jars, pour in as much good brandy as will percolate through the spaces not filled by the fruit. Renew as it becomes absorbed, until the liquor stands on top. Screw on the covers and leave for four months. Then turn the contents into a bowl; crush with a potato masher. Excellent for coughs and to serve as an after-dinner liqueur.

AUGUST 27TH

"My wife desired some damsons, and made me climb."—SHAKESPEARE ("Henry IV.").

DAMSONS should be either scalded and the skins removed or pricked in many places with a large needle. Weigh the fruit and allow to each pound three-quarters of a pound of sugar. Make a syrup by adding a cupful of water to each pound of sugar, and let it come to the boiling point. When it boils, skim it till clear and put in the plums a few at a time. When they are soft, lift them carefully into jars and let the syrup simmer gently for three-quarters of an hour, or until it has thickened to sufficient richness.

AUGUST 28TH

"She sat down in solitude to cold tea and the drum-sticks of the chicken."—MRS. GASKELL ("Wives and Daughters").

FOR chicken maître d'hôtel put into the chafing dish a tablespoonful of butter, and when hot add the chicken; cook until a light brown on each side; season with salt and paprika; squeeze over the meat the juice of a lemon; add a little parsley or watercress, and serve.

AUGUST 29TH

" 'Why, what am I a-thinking of!' said Toby. 'I shall forget my own name next. It's tripe!'"—CHARLES DICKENS ("The Chimes").

SOMETIMES tripe by another name is agreeable to those who have eaten it soggy, half-cooked, and cold, and still retain the gloomy recollection. Cooked as follows, they would not recognize it: Soak the tripe six hours, scrape clean, and simmer for three hours longer. Then cut it into dice and fry it in hot fat with some minced chives. Cover it with boiling water, add a couple of tomatoes, a stalk of celery, chopped, and a spoonful of chopped parsley, and stew gently for an hour, or until the tripe is perfectly tender. Season with salt and a little paprika, add a cup of hot cream thickened with flour to the sauce, and serve very hot.

AUGUST 30TH

"Salmon, lamb, peas, innocent young potatoes, a cool salad, sliced cucumber, a tender duckling— all there."—CHARLES DICKENS ("Martin Chuzzlewit").

SLICED cucumbers may be enjoyed all winter by preparing them when they are fresh after this recipe: Take two dozen large cucumbers and six small onions, pared and sliced very thin; place them in layers in a large jar, sprinkle salt on each layer. After standing six hours, drain thoroughly and cover with a dressing made of one cupful of olive oil, one quart of vinegar, one-half cupful each of white and black mustard seed and two tablespoonfuls of celery seed. Let it stand for twenty-four hours, and if necessary add vinegar enough to cover; put in jars and do not open for three or four months.

AUGUST 31ST

"Where other people would make preserves
He turns his fruit into pickles."—HOOD.

THE old-fashioned housekeeper frequently turned her fruit into pickles with excellent result. Peaches make on the whole the best sweet pickle, and the following is a good rule: Peel white peaches, and to every pound of fruit allow half a pound of sugar. Place sugar and fruit in a preserving kettle and bring to a boil. To three pounds of fruit allow one cup of vinegar and a tablespoonful each of mace, cinnamon, and cloves, tied up in little bags not to discolor the fruit. Pour the spiced vinegar over the fruit and boil fifteen minutes. Remove the fruit, and put it carefully into glass jars. Boil the syrup down until quite thick, pour over the fruit in the jars, and seal.

SEPTEMBER 1ST

"He . . . beat up yolks of eggs in neat Schiedam and administered it in small doses, followed this up by meat stewed in red wine and water, shredding into both mild febrifugal herbs that did no harm."—
CHARLES READE ("The Cloister and the Hearth").

AN egg cocktail is an excellent appetizer and more nourishing than its spirituous prototype. Mix for each cocktail a tablespoonful of lemon juice, a few drops of Tabasco sauce, a tablespoonful of sherry or Madeira, and a well-beaten egg. It should be served in a tall glass and eaten with a long-handled spoon.

SEPTEMBER 2D

"Nor hears with pain
New oysters cry'd, nor sighs for cheerful ale."
—JOHN PHILIPS.

WHEN the oysters are new each autumn and a fresh pleasure, the simplest method of preparing them seems best, and to those to whom raw oysters do not appeal an appetizing way to serve them is roasted in the shell. They need only be washed clean and laid upon hot coals or in a shallow pan on the top of the range, which should be hot. Lay the deeper shell next the pan; when they open wide, take off the loosened upper shell—be careful not to spill the juice—and lay upon a hot platter, with a small piece of butter on each. Pass pepper, salt, Tabasco, sliced lemon, and any other favorite sauce.

SEPTEMBER 3D

"If we will plant nettles, or sow lettuce."— SHAKESPEARE ("Othello").

SHRED two heads of green lettuce and cook for half an hour in a quart of chicken stock; rub through a colander and return to the fire; stir in two tablespoonfuls of butter rubbed into one of flour, a tablespoonful of chopped boiled onion, and a tablespoonful of minced parsley. In another sauce-pan heat, but do not boil, a cup of milk, seasoned with salt and pepper, stir in a well-whipped egg. Pour into the tureen and add the lettuce soup. Serve with strips of toast or crisp dinner biscuit.

SEPTEMBER 4TH

"We had delicate cucumbers stuffed with forced meats."—THACKERAY.

PARE the cucumbers and cut them in halves. Remove the seeds. Drop the cucumbers into cold salted water and set away in a cold place.

Make a forcemeat of breast of chicken, pounded to a paste, rubbed through a sieve, and cooked for ten minutes in a cupful of cream, with half a cupful of stale bread and seasoning of salt and pepper. A little onion juice is an improvement if the flavor of onion is liked. Wipe the cucumbers dry and fill with the forcemeat, packing it as much as possible. Stew in veal stock and serve with a sauce of the thickened stock.

SEPTEMBER 5TH

"After the puddings, sweet and black, the fritters and soup, came the third course, of which the chief dish was a hot venison pasty."—THACKERAY ("English Humourists").

TAKE the bones out of a shoulder of venison, season and beat the meat, cut it into large pieces, lay it in a stone jar, cover it with plain beef stock, set the jar in boiling water and let the contents simmer for three or four hours; then take it from the fire and set in a cold place until the next day. When ready to use remove the fat, lay the meat in a deep dish, season well, and cover with the stock gravy. Dot freely with lumps of butter and cover the dish with a thick biscuit crust. Bake in a moderate oven three-quarters of an hour.

SEPTEMBER 6TH

"Epicurean cooks sharpen with cloyless sauce his appetite."—SHAKESPEARE ("Antony and Cleopatra").

TO make chili sauce peel a peck of ripe tomatoes and half a dozen white onions. Chop fine and put over the fire to cook in their own juice half an hour. Strain through a sieve and add two cups of vinegar, a tablespoonful each of ground cinnamon, allspice, and black pepper, and a teaspoonful of cloves. Return to the fire and cook about four hours, or until it is quite thick, stirring often. When cooked sufficiently, add a tablespoonful of cayenne pepper, two teaspoonfuls of ground ginger, and two tablespoonfuls, or more, of salt. Bottle the sauce, cork and seal.

SEPTEMBER 7TH

"Oh those melons! If he's able
We're to have a feast! so nice!"
—BROWNING ("Soliloquy of the Spanish Cloister").

LAY cantaloupes or muskmelons on the ice till thoroughly chilled. Just before they are needed open them and remove the seeds. Slice in crescent-shaped pieces, cut off the rind and green part, leaving only the part that is quite ripe. Heap in a salad bowl with bits of ice and add a French dressing, or a mayonnaise may be used if a rich salad be desired.

SEPTEMBER 8TH

"Let the sky rain potatoes."—SHAKESPEARE ("Merry Wives of Windsor").

CUT into cubes one quart of cold potatoes. Put into a saucepan two scant tablespoonfuls of flour rubbed into two of butter; add one slice of onion, a little chopped parsley, a little salt and pepper, and a pint of milk. When hot pour a little at a time upon the potatoes. When the milk begins to boil move it back where it will only simmer, and let it cook five minutes. Season with a little more salt and pepper, and place in a shallow baking dish. Sprinkle over the top a cupful of grated bread crumbs and a tablespoonful of butter; bake in a rather hot oven for twenty minutes and serve promptly.

SEPTEMBER 9TH

"The next variation which their visit afforded was produced by the entrance of servants with cold meat, cake, and a variety of all the finest fruits in season."—JANE AUSTEN ("Pride and Prejudice").

A VERY good plain raisin cake is made by creaming together half a cup of butter and a cup and a quarter of sugar, then adding the beaten yolks of four eggs, a cup of water and about a quarter of a grated nutmeg. Take three cups of sifted flour in which has been stirred a full teaspoonful of baking-powder, sift again. Put part of the flour in a cupful of seeded raisins, stir into the egg and sugar mixture, add the beaten whites, stir lightly and fold in the remainder of the flour. Bake in a slow oven. If the eggs are large add a little more flour.

SEPTEMBER 10TH

"When I brought out the baked apples from the closet, and hoped our friends would be so very obliging as to take some, 'Oh!' said he, directly, 'there is nothing in the way of fruit half so good.'"—JANE AUSTEN ("Emma").

PARE and core apples tart but not sour; put in a pan with a very little water, fill the core holes with chopped English walnuts and a little sugar, and bake in a rather quick oven, basting often. When the apples are done, which will be when they can be pierced with a straw, set them away where they will get cold. Serve with whipped cream, sweetened and flavored with sherry.

SEPTEMBER 11TH

"Then came a kind of gruel and when the repast had lasted an hour or more some hashed meat highly peppered."—CHARLES READE ("The Cloister and the Hearth").

COLD beef of any kind, roast, steak, or pot roast, is excellent made into cecils and served with a brown or tomato sauce. Chop the beef fine, and to two cupfuls add a teaspoonful of onion juice, two tablespoonfuls of

fine dry bread-crumbs, and the yolks of
two eggs, and mix thoroughly. Add
one-fourth of a small nutmeg, grated
fine, a little salt, and a generous seasoning of paprika. Heat the mixture and
set aside to cool. When nearly cold,
make into balls the size of an English
walnut, roll in egg and then in bread-
crumbs, and fry in deep fat. Serve with
a brown sauce or one well-flavored with
tomato.

SEPTEMBER 12TH

"I'd a baking yesterday, Master Marner, and
the lard cakes turned out better nor common."—
GEORGE ELIOT ("Silas Marner").

THE " lard-cake " of old England
is the cruller of New England.
This old-fashioned recipe may be
trusted to produce a result " better nor
common." Five cupfuls of flour, one of
butter, two of sugar, four eggs, half a
grated nutmeg. Rub the butter and
sugar together, add the eggs, whites and
yolks beaten separately, then the flour.
Roll into a thin sheet, cut in narrow
strips with a jagging iron, twist into any
shape that commends itself, and fry in
a deep pot of *very* hot lard.

SEPTEMBER 13TH

"Some choice sous'd fish brought couchant in a dish."—CARTWRIGHT.

SOUSED mackerel can easily be prepared at home and is a great improvement on the canned variety. Clean and skin half a dozen small mackerel. Cut into convenient pieces and remove all the larger bones. Pack the fish in a stoneware, not earthenware, jar. Sprinkle with a quarter of a cupful of salt, a saltspoonful of paprika, half a cupful of whole mixed spices, cloves, peppercorns, and allspice in about equal quantities. Cover with vinegar. The salt and spices should be strewed on the fish as it is put in the jar. Cover and bake in a slow oven six hours. Take off the cover while it cools, then cover again. Keep in a cool place.

SEPTEMBER 14TH

"If thou tastest a crust of bread, thou tastest all the stars and all the heavens."—ROBERT BROWNING ("Paracelsus").

"PULLED bread" is a gastronomic blessing to the dyspeptic American. Take a loaf of fresh bread while it is still warm, break it in two and pull the soft part away from the crust in long strips of as even shape and size as possible. Place these on a biscuit-pan in the oven and bake to a light brown. Eaten before they are more than two days old they are deliciously nutty and crisp, and much more digestible than any other form of bread.

SEPTEMBER 15TH

"In due time the tea was spread forth in handsome style; and neither ham, tarts, nor marmalade were wanting among its accompaniments."—CHARLOTTE BRONTË ("Shirley").

PUT on to cook peeled and stoned peaches and allow them to simmer for three-quarters of an hour, stirring often. Then add sugar in the proportion of three-quarters of a pound to a pound of the fruit; allow it to boil a few minutes, skimming constantly. Then add the juice of a lemon to every two pounds of fruit and the chopped kernels of four peach-stones. Cook ten or fifteen minutes and fill glasses or marmalade jars.

SEPTEMBER 16TH

"He bid me taste of it; and 'twas the grape!"
—OMAR KHAYYAM ("Rubaiyat").

TO make grape-juice for the pleasant drink in vogue, wash, without stemming, Concord grapes. Put them over in a kettle with a cupful of cold water. When they have cooked till they are thoroughly soft, remove from the fire, and when cool enough strain and return to the fire with a cupful of sugar to each quart of juice. Let it boil while the scum rises and is removed. Have fruit cans standing in hot water, fill them till they overflow, cover tightly, and set in a cool place. The amount of sugar may be varied.

SEPTEMBER 17TH

"Have some more sauce to your leek? there is not enough leek to swear by."—SHAKESPEARE ("Henry V.").

A SAUCE in which the leek, or its sister, the onion, is very delicately present, is prepared by heating in a frying pan good dripping or butter, then frying in it several slices of onion. When they are well cooked remove them.

Put into the pan cold potatoes, cut in dice; cold young turnips or carrots; fry light brown, lift carefully from the fat. Serve very hot and dry in a hot dish.

SEPTEMBER 18TH

"There were eggs in napkins, and crispy bits of bacon under silver covers; and there were little fishes in a little box and devilled kidneys frizzling on a hot-water dish."—ANTHONY TROLLOPE ("The Warden").

CHOOSE plump veal or lamb kidneys; take out the hard centres and the fat; cut in slices half an inch thick. Heat together a tablespoonful of butter, a small teaspoonful of mustard, a good pinch of paprika, a little salt, and a good teaspoonful of lemon juice. In this dip each piece of kidney, roll in fine bread crumbs and broil; turn often. They should be done in eight or ten minutes. Serve on toast with the sauce poured over them.

SEPTEMBER 19TH

"Tarrant ventured to intimate that the apple fritters were very fine."—HENRY JAMES ("The Bostonians").

ALTHOUGH Mr. James has lived so long in England, he obviously has not forgotten all the pleasures of life in America. The apple fritter of New England is too well known to justify description, but the fritter from old England is a different matter, and to the taste of many quite as palatable. Cut French bread into thick squares. Soak these in cream flavored with nutmeg, powdered cinnamon and sugar and mixed with an egg. When the squares are well soaked fry them golden brown in very hot fat, spread them with butter and hot apple sauce.

SEPTEMBER 20TH

"He would keep recommending her to try the coarsest viands on the table; and at last, he told her if she could not fancy the cold beef to try a little with pickled onions."—MRS. GASKELL.

FOR pickling, choose small white onions, peel them, put into a pan of boiling water, a few at a time; when they look clear on the outside lift them carefully on to a cloth, cover with another; scald some more, and proceed as before. Let them lie till cold, then put them in jars and pour over them scalding white wine vinegar. When cold cover the jars.

SEPTEMBER 21ST

"A dish of wild fowl, that came afterward, furnished conversation for the rest of the dinner."— ADDISON ("Sir Roger de Coverley").

WILD fowl should be roasted without stuffing. The fishy taste that they sometimes have is removed by basting them with hot water, salted, in which an onion has been cooked. Toward the end baste them with butter only. A good sauce to serve with them is made by boiling a cupful of port wine, the same quantity of stock, a shallot and a bit of mace for ten minutes; add a tablespoonful of butter and a teaspoonful of flour, rubbed together; salt and pepper. Boil up once and serve.

SEPTEMBER 22D

"Where, on its bed
Of the orchard's black
Mould, the love-apple
Lies pulpy and red."
—Browning ("The Englishman in Italy").

SELECT large, smooth tomatoes (or "love-apples," as they used to be called). Cut out the core and fill the hollow space with a stuffing of minced chicken, bread crumbs, and chopped ripe olives. Spread a little butter over the top and cook half an hour in a moderately quick oven. There is no necessity of moistening the stuffing, as the juice of the tomato soon penetrates it.

SEPTEMBER 23D

"There are frogs cooking in it, no doubt."—
Thackeray.

THE hind legs of frogs are delicious, and should be fried in deep fat or fine olive oil till they are a light brown. Skin, wash, and soak in milk for twenty minutes; lift them out of the milk, pepper and salt them and coat with flour, then fry.

" Here, sweetheart, here's some green ginger for thee."—BEAUMONT and FLETCHER.

TRADITION has it that green ginger prepared in the following manner was a favorite preserve of Martha Washington: Scrape plump, smooth ginger root and throw into cold water. Allow eight pounds of sugar to seven of ginger. Bring it to the boil and let it boil steadily half an hour. Drain, put into fresh cold water and again bring it to the boil, allowing it to cook until tender. Make a preserving syrup in the proportion of eight pounds of sugar to two quarts of water. When this is cold, pour over the ginger; after two days pour off the syrup and boil it down, pouring it over the ginger again when cold. Repeat the process, this time pouring it hot over the ginger, which will now be permeated by it and will not shrink.

SEPTEMBER 25TH

"Enticing walnuts, I have known you well
In youth, when pickles were a passing pain."
—TAYLOR.

CHOOSE walnuts young and tender enough to be easily pierced with a needle. Pack them in jars, covering with good cider vinegar, poured on cold. Let them stand four months; pour off the vinegar and replace it with boiling vinegar, in which has been added to each quart an ounce of English mustard, a teaspoonful of horse-radish, a pinch of black pepper, cloves, and allspice, a teaspoonful of ginger and a tablespoonful of salt. Cover the jars closely, and do not use for three months more. They may be made without the spices, except pepper and salt. The vinegar first poured off is excellent for catsup or salads, having a good flavor.

SEPTEMBER 26TH

The plenteous pickle shall preserve the dish."—
GAY.

CHOOSE small cucumbers, and to half a peck of them add one pint of nasturtium pods, one quart each of string beans, small green tomatoes, and small white onions. Salt over night. In the morning add two ounces each of white and black mustard seed; two cauliflowers, boiled and cut up, half a pint of salt, half a pound of ground mustard, one gill of olive oil and four carrots, boiled tender and sliced. Cover the whole with scalding vinegar.

SEPTEMBER 27TH

"He doth learn to make strange sauces, to eat anchovies, macaroni, bovoli, fagioli, and caviare."
—BEN JONSON ("Cynthia's Revels").

BOIL a quarter of a pound of macaroni until tender; season it with salt and paprika and pour over it a tomato sauce made as follows:

Fry in a tablespoonful of butter a few leaves of parsley, a dozen fresh mushrooms, peeled and cut in small pieces, and an onion, sliced, or a clove of garlic (the latter gives the true Italian flavor). Add half a pint of hot water, in which three bouillon capsules have been dissolved, making a very strong stock, and a pint of canned tomatoes. Cook very gently for three hours. Strain, then stir in a lump of butter.

SEPTEMBER 28TH

"She went to the garden for parsley to stuff a rabbit."—SHAKESPEARE ("Taming of the Shrew").

TO make a rabbit taste like a hare, skin it and season it with black pepper and allspice. Pour over it a glass of port wine and the same amount of vinegar. Baste it with this occasionally, and after it has lain over night, stuff it with breadcrumbs, seasoned with salt, pepper, and chopped parsley, and roast in a moderate oven. Serve with a sauce of melted butter to which currant jelly has been added.

SEPTEMBER 29TH

"And my Barbary hen has laid two eggs; Heaven knows the trouble we had to bring her to it."—CHARLES READE ("Peg Woffington").

IF there is a little cold ham, boiled, fried or broiled, to be disposed of, chop it very fine and mix with the yolks of hard boiled eggs which have been removed from the whites and rubbed smooth. Put the mixture back in the whites, place them in a baking dish close together, pour over them a thick cream sauce, sprinkle dry bread crumbs on top, season with bits of butter, salt, and paprika, and bake long enough to brown nicely. Instead of chopped ham, the small cans of devilled ham may be used.

SEPTEMBER 30TH

"Though they could not all talk, they could all eat; and the beautiful pyramids of grapes, nectarines and peaches soon collected them around the table."—JANE AUSTEN ("Pride and Prejudice").

FRUIT used as a centrepiece is very handsome when dipped first into white of egg, lightly beaten, then in granulated sugar. Dry on a sieve and serve very cold on a bed of grape-leaves. Grapes, plums, and berries are the most adapted to this form of serving. Apples and peaches are best left with their blushing cheeks unadorned.

OCTOBER 1ST

"For the stock of clear soup you will get a leg of beef, a leg of veal and a ham."—THACKERAY ("A Little Dinner at Timmins's").

FOR good strong stock take three pounds of lean veal, three pounds of lean beef, one slice of ham or a ham-bone, two onions, two stalks of celery. Mince the ham or crack the ham-bone, put the meats and the seasoning over the fire in six quarts of cold water. Let this come slowly to the boiling point and then simmer for six or seven hours. Strain through a double cloth and set in a cold place. When the fat has hardened on top of the stock remove it carefully. Put the stock back on the fire with the unbeaten white and the shell of an egg. Let it heat quickly and boil fast for five minutes. Strain again. Add salt and pepper to taste just before serving. Many people like the addition of one glass of sherry.

OCTOBER 2D

"There were barrels of oysters, hecatombs of lobsters, a few tremendous-looking crabs and a tub full of pickled salmon."—ANTHONY TROLLOPE ("The Warden").

SOFT-SHELL crabs are good only when freshly caught, as the shells harden after twenty-four hours. Remove the sand-bags and the shaggy bits from the side; then wash and wipe; sprinkle with salt and pepper; roll in bread-crumbs, then in egg, then in crumbs; fry in smoking hot lard or, much better, in good olive oil.

OCTOBER 3D

"Enter a boiled turkey poult, with delicate white sauce."—CHARLES READE ("It Is Never Too Late To Mend").

A VERY delicate white sauce to serve with young turkey is egg-cream sauce, and is made by putting into a sauce-pan a large table-spoonful of butter and a heaping table-spoonful of flour, adding the flour a little at a time as the butter melts. As soon as butter and flour bubble, pour in two cups of cream and season with salt and green sweet peppers, chopped fine. Boil for a couple of minutes. Keep hot over boiling water; when ready to serve, put in three hard-boiled eggs, cut in small pieces.

OCTOBER 4TH

"Fanny must run down to Briarfield and buy some muffins and crumpets."—CHARLOTTE BRONTË ("Shirley").

CRUMPETS are not fashionable with the ordinary American baker, but they repay the trouble of making them at home. Put in a large bowl five cupfuls of sifted flour, a tablespoonful of sugar and a teaspoonful of salt.

Dissolve a quarter of a yeast-cake in a little luke-warm water, then add it to two cupfuls of warm water, pour on the flour and beat into a smooth batter. Cover and let stand over night. In the morning beat into the sponge three tablespoonfuls of melted butter. Let the mixture rise half an hour longer in a warm place, and bake in muffin-rings on a griddle.

OCTOBER 5TH

"The vulgar boil, the learned roast, an egg."—
POPE.

ONE can easily be learned enough to roast, or at least bake, an egg, and for this purpose come very convenient egg-bakers, of different sizes to suit the number of eggs. Butter the dish, allowing a tablespoonful of butter for four eggs; break the eggs carefully into the dish; set in rather cool oven until the white becomes set, but not hard. Season with salt, pepper, a little chopped parsley, and a few drops of onion juice, or, if there is a bit of cold ham in the house, a teaspoonful of that, chopped fine, on the top of each egg will vary the flavor.

OCTOBER 6TH

"Let onion atoms lurk within the bowl
And, half suspected, animate the whole."
—SIDNEY SMITH.

TO any of the green salads, where the ordinary French dressing is used, an agreeable variety is imparted by rubbing the salad-bowl with a piece of raw onion, or, if part of the company only like this addition, it is easy to regulate the matter by rubbing with onion the plates on which the salad is to be served.

OCTOBER 7TH

"Darling, hasten and prepare this turtle, it will be an addition to our meagre ordinary."—ROBERT LOUIS STEVENSON ("The Treasure of Franchard").

THE meat of a calf's head makes very good imitation turtle in place of the terrapin that is very expensive in our Northern markets. Boil the head until the meat drops from the bones; when cold cut the meat into small dice and put into a saucepan with an onion and some ham, also cut in dice; season with thyme, bay leaf, salt, pepper, and a wine-glass of Madeira or of good brandy; add a cup of Espagnole sauce or consommé, set on a good fire, and boil half an hour. Ten minutes before taking from the fire add two hard-boiled eggs, chopped fine, and the yellow rind of a lemon, also chopped.

OCTOBER 8TH

"Venison, game, pickles and provocatives in the centre of the table."—CHARLES READE ("Peg Woffington").

NO daintier "provocative" for an autumn dinner can be found than nasturtium sandwiches. Chop the seed-pods of the nasturtium vine, after having poured boiling vinegar on them and allowing them to cool in it. Mix with mayonnaise dressing and spread between thin slices of white bread. Garnish with nasturtium flowers, which also are good to eat, but too lovely for the sacrifice.

OCTOBER 9TH

"I can pay for my bread and cheese, and my nice little lodging, and my two coats a year."—WILKIE COLLINS ("The Moonstone").

ONE can lunch well on bread and cheese if the latter is combined with celery according to this rule: Boil in salted water until tender a head of celery cut into small pieces; drain and mix with a cupful of drawn butter, two ounces of grated cheese, and salt and pepper to taste. Bake in a shallow dish. Scatter grated cheese over the top, with a few bits of butter.

OCTOBER 10TH

"His sauce should be considered. Decidedly a few bread-crumbs, done up with his liver and brains and a dash of mild sage."—CHARLES LAMB ("Essays of Elia").

FROM our sauce for roast pig we will omit the brains, but will chop up the liver and add bread-crumbs together with a tablespoonful of powdered sage. Stir this into a generous quantity of melted butter, and serve in a gravy boat, with Charles Lamb's famous delicacy.

OCTOBER 11TH

"There, take . . . ye each a shell;
'Twas a fat oyster,—live—in peace—adieu."
—POPE.

A VERY nice oyster stuffing for a shoulder of mutton is described in an eighteenth century cookbook and turns out agreeable to the twentieth century taste, which is not the case with all antiquated dishes. A cupful of grated bread-crumbs, a piece of butter (suet in the old recipe), yolks of two hard-boiled eggs, a bit of onion, salt, pepper, thyme, and winter savory for seasoning, twelve oysters. Mix all the ingredients and bind together with the yolk of a raw egg.

OCTOBER 12TH

"The two doctors were for keeping him on gruel, lemonade, barley-water and so on."—WILKIE COLLINS ("The Moonstone").

FOR a barley-water that is agreeable as well as wholesome, boil two pounds of lean veal in one quart of water; add to it a quarter of a pound of pearl barley and boil until it can be rubbed through a sieve; add salt.

OCTOBER 13TH

"And luscious scallops to allure the taste
Of rigid zealots to delicious fasts."—GAY.

SCALLOPS, like oysters, are handsomest when large and most delectable when small. To eat them at their best, dip them in a batter made of a pint of flour, two eggs beaten light, and half a pint of milk, with a teaspoonful of salt for seasoning. Drop spoonfuls of the scallops and batter into boiling fat. The batter makes a shell about them in which they are practically steamed, and this shell may easily be discarded by those averse to fried food. The scallop itself thus cooked is not difficult of digestion.

OCTOBER 14TH

"Moore had risen before the sun and had taken a ride to Whinbury and back ere his sister had made the café au lait or cut the tartines for his breakfast."
—CHARLOTTE BRONTË ("Shirley").

THE tartines of America to-day, if not of Charlotte Brontë's England, are prepared in many ways, one of the best and simplest being to spread thin slices of Boston brown bread first with butter and then with cream, or pot cheese. Sprinkle thickly with sweet green peppers chopped fine and moistened with a few drops of lemon juice. Cut the slices in halves and press the two halves together.

OCTOBER 15TH

"A man may feel thankful, heartily thankful, over a dish of plain mutton with turnips . . . when he shall confess a perturbation of mind inconsistent with the purposes of the grace, at the presence of venison or turtle."—CHARLES LAMB.

AS an accompaniment for mutton a purée of turnips is sometimes welcome. Cook until tender pared and sliced turnips in salted boiling water. Press through a colander; add a tablespoonful of butter rubbed in one of flour; pepper and salt, and a half cupful of cream heated with a tiny bit of soda. When it has all boiled up once, take from the fire and stir in a beaten egg. Do not let it boil again, but set the saucepan in boiling water for a few minutes, stirring occasionally.

OCTOBER 16TH

"Have a munch of grouse and a hunk of bread."
—ROBERT BROWNING ("Donald").

CUT the meat from the breast of a plump grouse; break up the carcass into small pieces, put into a saucepan with two tablespoonfuls of chopped bacon, a chopped onion, four whole cloves, a little mace and a small bay leaf, a little parsley and a stalk of celery, a peppercorn and one minced carrot. Add three cups of stock and simmer for two hours. Strain and skim off the fat. Cook the pieces of breast in butter, or olive-oil, to a light brown on each side; add the sauce, a little salt, and a gill of claret, and simmer for five minutes.

OCTOBER 17TH

"A most sharp sauce—and is it not well served into a sweet goose?"—SHAKESPEARE ("Romeo and Juliet").

A SAUCE sharp enough for a sweet goose or any other amiable fowl is made with one cupful of brown stock, two tablespoonfuls of butter, one tablespoonful of flour, two tablespoonfuls of chopped capers, two tablespoonfuls of vinegar, one tablespoonful of chopped chives, one teaspoonful of sugar, one-half teaspoonful of salt, a little cayenne pepper. Brown the butter, rub the flour into it, then add the stock and the other ingredients; cook for ten minutes, stirring constantly.

OCTOBER 18TH

"I eat a palatable fig."—ROBERT BROWNING ("Ferishtah's Fancies").

SOAK dried pulled figs in cold water for some hours, then stew them until they swell. Lift them carefully on to the dish in which they are to be served; let them cool and arrange around them whipped cream, flavored with sherry, maraschino, or essence of almond and slightly sweetened with powdered sugar.

OCTOBER 19TH

"Pudding our parson eats, the squire loves hare, But white-pot thick is my Buxoma's fare."
—GAY.

WHITE bean soup, or "white-pot," as it used to be called, is both nourishing and delicious made as follows: Soak one cupful of white beans over night in plenty of water. In the morning put them in a soup pot with three quarts of cold water. Cook for five hours. Strain through a sieve, rubbing the beans through as thoroughly as possible; add salt, white pepper, a large tablespoonful of butter, and a cup of cream; also a teaspoonful of celery salt. Cook twenty minutes. Serve with croutons of bread.

OCTOBER 20TH

"Tidbury drank water with his meals, if meals those miserable scraps of bread and cheese, or bread and sausage, could be called, which he lined his lean stomach with."—THACKERAY.

CHOP a pound and a half of pork and the same of veal, cleared of skin and sinews, and three-quarters of a pound of beef suet; mince and mix them; steep the crumb of a penny loaf in water and mix it with the meat. Season with dried sage, salt, and pepper. This is an old English recipe.

OCTOBER 21ST

"I can teach sugar to slip down your throat in a million ways."—DEKKER and FORD.

ADD to the white of an egg an equal quantity of very strong black coffee, then stir in as much confectioner's sugar as you can and keep the mixture soft enough to mould. When it is a smooth paste, roll small pieces between the palms, making little balls; press between halves of English walnuts, removed from the shells without breaking.

OCTOBER 22D

"I will make an end of my dinner,
There's pippins and cheese to come."
—SHAKESPEARE ("Merry Wives of Windsor").

A FINE hot dessert for a cool day is made by enclosing each tart pippin in a crust of puff paste, baking in a slow oven, and sprinkling with sugar ten or fifteen minutes before taking them out. Serve a sauce of thick cream, sugar, and nutmeg to pour over them, and have a cream cheese to eat with them.

OCTOBER 23D

"Hovering mute and inaccessible on the outskirts of æsthetic tea."—CARLYLE ("Sartor Resartus").

TO have tea that is truly "æsthetic" in taste and appearance, make it precisely as drip-coffee is made. The tea should be placed in a fine strainer, such as comes with the French coffee-pots, the strainers occasionally sold with teapots having too coarse holes for the purpose. Pour boiling water through the tea, then pour it back over the leaves a second time. Tea should always be served in a china teapot finished on the inside with a hard glaze, the porous earthenwares invariably becoming after a short time impregnated with the tannic-acid flavor.

OCTOBER 24TH

"Yon shapeless nothing in a dish." — COWPER ("Poems").

PLACE in a shallow dish sponge or other plain cake, and rather close together stick blanched almonds in regular rows. Pour over it half a pint of warm custard, a spoonful at a time, and set away to cool. Eat cold, with whipped cream, sweetened slightly and flavored, or with cold custard. This old-fashioned dessert is known as Hedgehog Trifle, and if the almonds are left standing pretty well out of the cake, its appearance justifies its name.

OCTOBER 25TH

"'Something ails my gracious master,' cried the keeper of the seal. 'Sure, my lord, it is the lampreys served at dinner, or the veal.'"—THACKERAY ("Rebecca and Rowena").

THE ancient Worcester way of cooking lampreys was to remove the cartilage which runs down the back, after cleaning carefully, and season with a little salt, cloves, mace, nutmeg, pepper, and allspice; put in a small saucepan with very strong beef gravy, port wine, and an equal quantity of sherry or Madeira.

OCTOBER 26TH

"A hundred souls of turkeys in a pie."—POPE.

IF turkey is to be served in a pie, pull the meat from the breast instead of cutting it, and put it into a baking-dish with a sauce made of white stock, slightly thickened, a cup of cream, and a piece of butter the size of an egg. Cook slowly for two hours, keeping the dish covered. Then add twenty-five oysters, cover with a pastry crust, and cook until brown. The meat of the upper joints may be included if desired.

OCTOBER 27TH

"Good worts! good cabbage." — SHAKESPEARE ("Merry Wives of Windsor").

CUT the cabbage in large pieces and cook until tender; change the water once. Pour off the water, and when perfectly cold chop fine, season with paprika and salt, and put into a saucepan with a cup of hot milk or hot stock. Cook till most of the liquid is cooked away; stir in a tablespoonful of melted butter and the juice of a lemon, and serve.

OCTOBER 28TH

"Pippin of my own grafting, with a dish of cara-ways."—SHAKESPEARE ("Henry IV.").

CORE and pare some pippins; put in a shallow dish, the bottom of which is covered with water. Fill the cavities with sugar, mixed with grated lemon peel and a few caraway seed. Bake in a quick oven, basting often with the syrup.

OCTOBER 29TH

"Caroline . . . hastened to hand to her uncle's vast, revered, and, on the whole, worthy friend, a glass of wine and a plate of macaroons." —CHARLOTTE BRONTË ("Shirley").

TO make macaroons, blanch, dry, and pound to a paste half a pound of almonds, with one teaspoonful of rose-water. Beat together the whites of three eggs and half a cupful of powdered sugar, adding the sugar slowly.

Put in half a teaspoonful of almond essence, then the pounded almonds, and add a tablespoonful of flour, if it is too soft to be shaped without. Roll with wet hands to the size of a walnut, flatten, place on buttered paper, and bake slowly.

OCTOBER 30TH

"Mild and dulcet as the flesh of young pigs."—CHARLES LAMB ("Essays of Elia").

UNLIKE other broiled meats, pork tenderloin should be cooked several minutes before it is eaten. Broil over a good fire for about twenty to twenty-five minutes, turn every two minutes. Lay upon a hot dish, sprinkle with salt and pepper and with lemon juice, and dot here and there with bits of butter. Cover closely and allow to stand for ten minutes before serving. Hot unsweetened apple-sauce should be passed with this dish, indigestible but good.

OCTOBER 31ST

"A collection of cooling refreshments,—wine, fruit, cakes."—CHARLOTTE BRONTË ("Shirley").

TO make nut wafers, cream a quarter of a cup of butter, beat in one egg and one cup of sugar, and keep beating till smooth. Add a scant teaspoonful of vanilla, or half a teaspoonful of almond extract, and a cupful of chopped nuts. Then stir in one cup of well-sifted flour in which has been mixed a small teaspoonful of baking powder. Drop in small spoonfuls on a buttered pan and bake in hot oven.

NOVEMBER 1ST

"A smoking soup, here came in, borne by the smiling host. 'Behold a *potage* of my fashion!' says my landlord, laying down the dish."—THACKERAY ("The Virginians").

FOR pepper-pot soup, to three quarts of water put vegetables according to the season—in summer, peas, lettuce, and spinach; in winter, carrots, turnips, celery, and onions at any time of year. Cut them small and stew with two pounds of the neck of mutton or with a fowl till quite tender. On first boiling, skim. Half an hour before serving add the meat of a lobster. Season with salt and cayenne pepper. A small quantity of rice should be put in with the meat. This is an old-fashioned English recipe, and is very good, very rich, and very warming on a bitter night in winter when cold blows the blast.

NOVEMBER 2D

"Nobody ever dreamed such soup as was put upon the table directly afterwards; or such fish; or such side-dishes; or such a top and bottom; or such a course of birds and sweets." — CHARLES DICKENS ("Martin Chuzzlewit").

THERE are many people to whom the delights of codfish tongues are unknown, but they are a great delicacy. Wash a dozen or more; put them over the fire in cold water, a table-spoonful of salt, a sliced onion, and half a lemon, sliced. Let them come to a boil quickly; when they have boiled one minute, set them away to cool in an earthenware dish in the water they were boiled in. When cool dip them in milk, roll them in sifted bread-crumbs, then fry them in hot butter till they are a delicate brown, turning them as they brown. Serve them with tomato or other piquant sauce.

NOVEMBER 3D

"Soon he and Gerard and Margaret were supping royally on broiled venison."—CHARLES READE ("The Cloister and the Hearth").

A VENISON steak is cut from the leg or from the shoulder-blade, the latter having a superior flavor. Broil rare, and serve with a sauce made by melting a tablespoonful of currant jelly in a glassful of hot Madeira, to which a teaspoonful of lemon juice has been added. Pepper and salt the steak lightly before pouring the sauce over it.

NOVEMBER 4TH

"Fetch up the venison and the sweet sauce,— you may leave the water gruel till I ring for it." —CHARLES READE ("It Is Never Too Late To Mend").

CURRANT-JELLY sauce is an old favorite to serve with venison or mutton. To one tablespoonful of butter add one of flour, browned in the oven; cook together till they bubble and begin to darken, when a cupful of consommé or brown soup-stock should be poured in slowly. To darken still more add a few drops of caramel. Just before taking from the fire stir in half a cup of currant jelly.

NOVEMBER 5TH

"Hares, pheasants, partridges, snipes, barn-door chickens (those 'tame villatic fowl'), capons, plovers, brawn, barrels of oysters, I dispense as freely as I receive them."—CHARLES LAMB ("Essays of Elia").

CUT off the breast from half a dozen snipe. Put in a frying pan a tablespoonful of butter, rub into it a teaspoonful of flour till brown and smooth. Add two cloves, a peppercorn, a sprig of parsley, a gill of water, a gill of claret, and a tablespoonful of chopped mushrooms. Cover the pan and simmer for two minutes after adding the breasts of the snipe. Spread thin slices of toast with currant jelly, and on these serve the snipe, pouring the gravy over them.

NOVEMBER 6TH

"Those unctuous morsels of deer's flesh were not made to be received with dispassionate services. I hate a man who swallows it, affecting not to know what he is eating."—CHARLES LAMB.

A VENISON ragout may be made as unctuous as one pleases from pieces unsuitable to use as steaks. Cut the meat into large squares, put it into a frying pan with hot butter, and toss it about for not more than five minutes. Add a tablespoonful of flour, then a pint of brown stock, half a cupful of mushrooms, a tablespoonful of currant jelly, and a little salt. Pepper and onion juice, which are usually advised, are best omitted. Mushrooms combine particularly well with the venison flavor.

NOVEMBER 7TH

"But Messenger was carving a loin of veal. Jem Messenger sat opposite him, eating bacon and beans on a very large scale."—CHARLES READE ("Clouds and Sunshine").

AS an agreeable variation from pork and beans, boil and rub through a colander a quart of white beans. Heat in a saucepan a large teaspoonful of butter, with paprika, salt, a teaspoonful of sugar, a tablespoonful of chopped parsley, and a leaf or two of mint, chopped fine. Stir in the beans and toss and stir constantly till very hot. Place on a hot platter with bits of bacon around the edge.

NOVEMBER 8TH

"Soupe à la bonne femme with a *perdrix aux choux* to follow, and pancakes and *fromage de Brie,* and to drink a bottle of *Romané Conti."*—GEORGE DU MAURIER ("Peter Ibbetson").

TO make the French pancakes referred to above, beat whites and yolks of three eggs separately, and to the yolks add a cup of milk, half a teaspoonful of salt and a teaspoonful of sugar. Pour one-third of this mixture on half a cupful of flour and beat till smooth; add the remainder of the milk, beat well, and put in a dessertspoonful of salad oil and the whites of the eggs. Heat and butter a small frying pan, cover with a thin layer of the batter; brown and turn. When a light brown on each side, spread quickly with butter and a tart jelly, roll and sprinkle with powdered sugar in which has been stirred a little ground cinnamon.

NOVEMBER 9TH

"Don't get any dainties for me, my dear; bread and cheese is the chief of my diet."—MRS. GASKELL ("Wives and Daughters").

BREAD and cheese combined make an excellent luncheon or supper dish known as baked Welsh rabbit. Have ready a cupful and a half of bread crumbs free from crusts and a cupful of grated rich cheese, about a cupful of milk and two tablespoonfuls of butter. Put in a baking-dish a layer of bread-crumbs, strew with bits of butter, a little salt, a dust of paprika, then a layer of cheese. Repeat till the dish is full; then pour on enough milk to moisten well, but not soak, the bread-crumbs. Sprinkle dry crumbs on top with plenty of bits of butter. Bake in a quick oven.

NOVEMBER 10TH

"Look at me! I make my own bread, and there's no difference between one batch and another from year's end to year's end; but if I'd got any other woman besides Vixen in the house, I must pray to the Lord every baking to give me patience if the bread turned out heavy."—GEORGE ELIOT ("Adam Bede").

A CAREFUL rule for home-made bread is this: Late in the evening place in bread-pan three quarts of sifted flour and a teaspoonful of salt. Soak half a cake of compressed yeast in a cupful of lukewarm water; add two quarts of water of the same temperature and mix well into the flour. Cover the pan with a clean cloth, and the bread board, and set it to rise where the temperature is 70 or 75 degrees. In

the morning add flour enough to make
a fairly stiff dough. Knead half an hour,
then set it by the fire for five hours. Separate into loaves. Knead them ten minutes and set to rise again. When light,
bake in a quick oven.

NOVEMBER 11TH

"Take a dejeune of muskadel and eggs."—BEN
JONSON ("The New Inn").

TO make "egg wine," as it is
called in the annals of old English
cookery, beat an egg, mix with it
a tablespoonful of cold water. Set on
the fire a glass of muskadel, half a glass
of water, a little sugar, and a grating
of nutmeg. When it boils, pour over the
beaten egg slowly, stirring well; return
it to the fire where it will not be too hot,
stirring it one way, for not more than
a minute. If it boils, or the egg is not
fresh, it will curdle.

NOVEMBER 12TH

"Oats for their feasts the Scottish shepherds
give."—GAY.

TO make a fine oatmeal caudle
take three quarts of boiling water,
add a pint of cold water into
which has been stirred until smooth six

tablespoonfuls of oatmeal; cook until it thickens, then season with a little salt, a dash of pepper, and sweeten to taste. Add a half pint of ale and a small wineglass of gin. The old rule for this caudle tells us that it will be of "incalculable service" to the sick and weak.

NOVEMBER 13TH

"I myself, and not another, would eat her nice cake."—CHARLES LAMB ("Essays of Elia").

A PLEASANT and deceptive reminiscence of New England loaf cake is furnished by "no egg cake," which is a useful recipe for times and seasons when eggs are scarce and high. Cream one-half a cupful of butter with one cupful of sugar; stir in a cupful of milk and one of raisins, stoned and dredged with flour; flavor with a teaspoonful of vanilla, a little nutmeg, and a pinch of cinnamon; at the last stir lightly in two and a half cupfuls of sifted flour in which is well mixed three teaspoonfuls of baking-powder. Other flavoring may be substituted, or added, but a mixture of flavors is best.

NOVEMBER 14TH

"What will this sister of mine do with rice?"—
SHAKESPEARE ("Winter's Tale").

RICE served as a vegetable is improved by browning in melted butter after it has been carefully cooked without stirring in a double boiler. If the rice is the excellent South Carolina variety it will come out when perfectly tender with every grain unbroken. Stir into it as lightly as possible a tablespoonful of chives before browning. Heap on a platter and serve very hot.

NOVEMBER 15TH

"I have ordered twelve sorts of fish at the 'Peacock,' my Lord."—CHARLES READE ("Peg Woffington").

IN a collection of twelve fish the old-fashioned smoked sturgeon ought to have a place. Cut it in steaks about an inch thick and broil it over charcoals. Rub butter and lemon juice over it in liberal quantities and eat with hot muffins, fried potatoes, and watercress for a Sunday morning breakfast.

NOVEMBER 16TH

"I'm blest if he didn't bring master a plate of cabbitch!" — THACKERAY ("The Yellowplush Papers").

THE delicate variety of cabbage known as Brussels sprouts is much improved by careful cooking. The sprouts should be thoroughly washed and then thrown into an abundance of boiling water and boiled for eight minutes; then drained and thrown into cold water; drain again and cook for fifteen or twenty minutes in a large cupful of boiling veal stock. Before serving add salt and pepper and two tablespoonfuls of cream, and pour the stock into the dish with the sprouts.

NOVEMBER 17TH

"There was a hot shoulder of mutton and onion sauce."—THACKERAY.

TO prepare onion sauce peel the onions and boil until tender; drain, chop fine and add them to a rich white sauce, boil up once and serve with the meat. A turnip boiled with the onions, but not served, improves the flavor.

NOVEMBER 18TH

"If my Master has given me ten talents, my duty is to trade with them and make them ten talents more Not in the dust of household drawers shall the coin be interred—least of all will I hide it in a tureen of cold potatoes to be ranged with bread, butter pastry and ham on the shelves of the larder."
—CHARLOTTE BRONTË ("Shirley").

A USE for cold potatoes, of which no one need speak slightingly, is to make them into a salad, alone or in combination. Slice rather thin six or eight good-sized potatoes; add a teaspoonful of chopped parsley, a tablespoonful of capers or chopped cucumber pickle, and marinade with three tablespoonfuls of vinegar and six of oil, a teaspoonful of salt, one-quarter of teaspoonful of pepper, and one teaspoonful of onion juice. Set in a cold place for an hour or more. A little celery, cut in small bits, may be added and the onion omitted. Serve on lettuce leaves.

"For the more genteel,
Snipe, woodcock, partridge, pheasant, quail we'll
serve."—W. CARTWRIGHT ("The Ordinary").

RUB the snipe inside and out with a wet cloth instead of washing. After scalding a minute in hot water, skin the lower legs, cut off the feet, skin the head, and remove the eyes. Wrap each one in a thin slice of bacon or salt pork and bake in a hot oven; baste well with butter. Chop livers and hearts very fine, season with salt, pepper, onion juice, and butter; heat very hot, spread on small slices of toast, and place for a moment in the oven. Remove from the oven, pour over the toast the juice from the baking-pan, put the birds on the toast and serve hot.

NOVEMBER 20TH

"Right glad he was to find a caldron full of gelatinized beef soup."—CHARLES READE ("It Is Never Too Late to Mend").

FOR beef soup the "top of the sirloin" is excellent; it is better than the round, as it has richer flavor. Whatever beef is selected, remove all the fat and cut it in small pieces. Barely cover it with water, let it boil up rapidly, and then add cold water in the proportion of one quart of water to each pound of meat. Flavor it with a mince of carrots, turnips, and other roots and herbs. When it has cooked one hour, add a scant cupful of well-washed rice. A cupful of stewed tomatoes, a few mushrooms, or almost any other vegetable may be added to beef broth to its improvement. If this broth has been properly cooked, which means being allowed to simmer for three hours, the meat will literally melt in the mouth, the fibre being thoroughly weakened and the nutriment well distributed.

NOVEMBER 21ST

"It was a glorious supper. There were kippered salmon, and Finnan haddock, and a lamb's head, and a haggis."—CHARLES DICKENS ("Pickwick Papers").

FINNAN haddock or "haddie," as it is commonly called, makes an excellent plain dish for Sunday night tea as a "relish," or for breakfast served with eggs. Wash the fish thoroughly, leave in cold water half an hour, then bring to the boil in order to soften them slightly. Wipe dry, rub over with butter and lemon-juice, and broil fifteen minutes. Serve on a hot covered dish.

"There were five mince-pies. Mr. Pendennis!
You saw yourself there were five went away from
table yesterday."—THACKERAY ("The Newcomes").

THE following recipe for mince-
meat has been used in one family
for nearly fifty years, and three
generations have sung its praises. The
materials required are three large cupfuls of finely chopped beef, boiled very
tender; six cupfuls of chopped apples;
one cupful of molasses; one tablespoonful of cinnamon, one of allspice, and
half a tablespoonful of cloves; one nutmeg, grated; two tablespoonfuls of salt,
chopped peel of two lemons, two cupfuls
of sugar, one quart of hard cider, juice
and pulp of an orange and a lemon, half
a pound of currants, half a pound of
raisins, a quarter of a pound of sliced
citron, a cupful of brandy. Mix all the
ingredients together and boil them half
an hour. Turn the mixture into a stone
crock, cover with a white cloth tied down
to exclude dust, and a tin cover or
a plate on top of this. In a cool place it
will keep for months. The pie-crust will
be more wholesome, though less flaky, if
made with butter in place of lard.

NOVEMBER 23D

" 'Tis the sour sauce to the sweet meat."—DRYDEN ("To Etheridge").

THE best tart sauce to eat with meat, particularly poultry, is made of cranberries. In one pint of cold water put one quart of the berries; cook slowly till broken to pieces, when they should be removed from the fire and put through a colander. Add the sugar, return to the fire, and cook just long enough to have the sugar dissolve.

NOVEMBER 24TH

"Nothing but barons of beef and turkeys would go down with him,—to the great greasing and detriment of his new sackcloth bib and tucker."— CHARLES LAMB.

TO prepare a stuffed boiled turkey, mix with one quart of breadcrumbs half a head of celery, chopped fine; two scant tablespoonfuls of salt, half a teaspoonful of pepper, two heaping tablespoonfuls of butter, and two eggs. Stuff the turkey with this, sew up and truss. Wring a square cloth out of cold water and dredge it thickly with flour. Pin the turkey in this and plunge into boiling water. Let it boil rapidly for fifteen minutes, then set back where it will simmer. Allow three hours for a turkey weighing nine pounds. Serve with celery sauce.

NOVEMBER 25TH

"One would not, like Lear, 'give everything.' I make my stand upon pig."—CHARLES LAMB.

ALTHOUGH fewer people than formerly "make their stand upon pig," one form or another of pork is frequently used to make variety in plain bills of fare. An old-fashioned dish that still can count its appreciative partakers is "fried pork and apples," a very rich and palatable combination. Fry five or six slices of pork until about half done, then lift them out of the fat and put them in another frying-pan to finish cooking. To the fat in the first pan add thick slices of apples, cored but not peeled, and stew until tender. A more delicate dish is made by substituting butter for pork fat and serving the apples with thin slices of broiled bacon.

NOVEMBER 26TH

"In after-dinner talk
Across the walnuts and the wine."
—TENNYSON ("The Miller's Daughter").

BOIL together one cupful each of granulated sugar and boiling water for half an hour. Then dip the point of a skewer into the syrup and then into cold water. If the thread formed is brittle the syrup is ready. Do not stir, and boil slowly and steadily. When done set the kettle in boiling water. Take shelled walnuts on the point of a skewer and dip into the syrup, and lay on a lightly buttered dish to harden.

NOVEMBER 27TH

"We'll try whether Matthew or I shall get the largest cut of the apple-pie to-day."—CHARLOTTE BRONTË ("Shirley").

THE apple-pie of our grandmothers was worth fighting over. These skilful ladies made a very short pie-crust of lard cut into sifted flour and wet into paste with ice-water. This they rolled out in a long, narrow strip, dabbed with butter, rolled together, and, standing it on edge, rolled it out flat again. For the upper crust this process was three times repeated. They filled the pie heaping full with tart, juicy apples, sliced, and buttered the edges of the under crust before laying on the upper crust. When the pie was baked this upper crust was deftly lifted off and a lump of butter, some sugar, and nutmeg were stirred into the apple filling. The crust was replaced and the pie eaten.

NOVEMBER 28TH

"'Ye might ha' made the parridge worse,' she said to Dinah; 'I can ate it wi'out its turnin' my stomach. It might ha' been a trifle thicker an' no harm, an' I allays putten a sprig o' mint in mysen; but how's ye t' know that?' " — GEORGE ELIOT ("Adam Bede").

A REALLY good porridge is not to be despised, either in sickness or health. If it is for an invalid the following rule is a good one: Wash a tablespoonful of rice and boil in a pint of water for fifteen minutes; add a pint of milk, in which a tablespoonful of flour has been stirred smooth; mix the flour with two or three spoonfuls of the milk before adding it to the remainder. Cook for an hour in a double boiler, season with a teaspoonful of salt. The same rule, with double the amount of milk, a dash of red pepper, and a little onion juice, makes excellent rice soup.

NOVEMBER 29TH

"At the sides was spinage, and pudding made hot."—GOLDSMITH.

WASH with great care a peck of spinach, put into a saucepan with half a cup of cold water and cook for twenty minutes to half an hour after it begins to boil. Salt the spinach, then turn into a colander to drain; mince fine. Heat a large tablespoonful of butter, stir into it a scant tablespoonful of flour, and when hot add salt and pepper and stir into the spinach; when it comes to a boil add four tablespoonfuls of cream and stir constantly for a few minutes. Garnish with hard-boiled egg, and serve on slices of toast. This is a pleasant variation from the usual way of serving.

"Our honest neighbour's goose and dumplings were fine."—GOLDSMITH ("Vicar of Wakefield").

THIS undoubtedly was stewed green goose, which is almost as delicate as spring chicken. A good recipe for a green-goose stew requires two of the young birds, which should be washed and cleaned and highly seasoned with salt, pepper, mace, and allspice. Put one bird inside the other, and press them as close together as possible, drawing the legs inward. Put them in a baking-pan, with a cupful of water, spread a tablespoonful of butter over them and bake in a slow oven. The dumplings are raised with yeast instead of baking-powder, the dough being made as for bread, but with milk in place of water. Let it rise an hour before the fire, then make into balls the size of a small apple, and drop them into boiling water. Twenty minutes of fast boiling will cook them. On serving, tear each dumpling slightly apart with two forks, to let the steam escape and prevent their becoming heavy.

"Dame Best . . . has had soup and pudding from the Hall every day; and once she went so far as to say it was not altogether a bad pudding."—CHARLES READE ("Peg Woffington").

A SOUP that is judged on its merits as to nourishing and appetizing qualities, and not on its appearance, is a plain vegetable soup, whose base is a good stock made the day before it is needed of odds and ends of cooked and uncooked meats, allowing a quart of water to each pound of meat and bone. Cook slowly till the liquid is reduced about one-half; set away to cool, and when quite cold remove the fat which will have risen to the top in a cake. Two hours before the soup is needed put the stock on where it will heat slowly and add to it a carrot chopped fine, two or three onions, tomatoes, celery stocks or roots, green peas, or any convenient vegetable, with half a cup of well-washed rice. Season rather highly, and do not strain out the vegetables.

DECEMBER 2D

" 'Capital,' said he. His mouth was full of it; his face quite red with the delightful exercise of gobbling. 'Mother, it's as good as my own curries in India.' "—THACKERAY ("Vanity Fair").

PUT into a pan an ounce of butter, stir over the fire until it melts, add a teaspoonful of minced white onion; when brown add a heaping teaspoonful of curry powder, the meat from the tails of two boiled lobsters, the juice of half a lemon, a teaspoonful of browned flour, and a pint of clear soup stock or hot water; simmer until it thickens; add a saltspoonful of salt, and serve. This is a mild curry.

DECEMBER 3D

"A pasty costly made
Where quail and pigeon, lark and leveret lay,
Like fossils of the rock, with golden yolks
Imbeddied and injellied."
—TENNYSON ("Audley Court").

DRAW the quails and wipe them outside and in with a damp cloth. Put a raw oyster or two in each quail. Fasten slices of bacon, cut very thin, over the breast; put them in a pan with a little hot water, cover closely, and cook twenty to twenty-five minutes, according to the size, in a rather hot oven. Baste occasionally, and at the last uncover for five minutes. Season with butter, salt, and pepper, and serve on squares of buttered toast moistened with gravy from the pan.

DECEMBER 4TH

"I'll make her a pudding, and a pudding she'll like, too. . . . Many a one has been comforted in their sorrow by seeing a good dish come upon the table."—MRS. GASKELL ("Cranford").

A REASONABLY comforting pudding for a winter day, which requires, however, an appetite somewhat sturdier than is expected of the sorrowful, is made by pouring over half a pint of fine bread-crumbs half a pint of scalding milk, adding, after an hour, four beaten eggs, a teaspoonful of flour, an ounce of butter, two ounces of sugar, half a pound of currants, an ounce of powdered almonds, half an ounce of shredded citron, the same of lemon peel, and a quarter of a teacupful of French brandy. Mix and tie tightly in a floured cloth and place in a buttered pudding-dish, that should be of a size precisely to fit it. Boil an hour. Serve with a hard sauce.

DECEMBER 5TH

"Clouted cream so seldom comes to London quite fresh."—CHARLES READE ("Peg Woffington").

EVERY housekeeper may have Devonshire cream on her own table if she will take the trouble to prepare it. Rich new milk is put in a very shallow vessel, which is set on the range, where the milk will be warmed, but on no account must it boil or even scald. The cream will rise to the surface in a short time, and the pan is then taken off and placed in the ice-box. When thoroughly chilled the cream may be skimmed, and it will be found very thick. Put it in a jar and use for cereals, berries, everything that ordinary cream is used for, its merit being that it is the richest of cream and also that it will keep for several days.

DECEMBER 6TH

"He managed a couple of plates full of strawberries and cream, and twenty-four little rout cakes that were lying neglected in a plate near him."—THACKERAY ("Vanity Fair").

TO make the little rout cakes famous in English literature since the eighteenth century, mix two pounds of flour, one of butter, one of sugar, one of clean, dry currants; wet into a stiff paste with two eggs, a table-spoonful each of orange-flower water, rose-water, sweet wine, and brandy; drop on floured tin plates and bake in a quick oven.

DECEMBER 7TH

"She wrenched from her brow a diamond and eyed it with contempt, took from her pocket a sausage and contemplated it with respect and affection."
—CHARLES READE ("Peg Woffington").

IF one likes the flavor of sausage, but finds it rather too "porky" as it comes from market, an easy expedient is to buy the best sausage-meat obtainable—not the links—and add to it as much more lean chopped beef; make into cakes and cook thoroughly in a very hot pan, turning often not to burn.

DECEMBER 8TH

"Maria is ready for you now in the kitchen, Mrs. Morrell, the onions have come."—BERNARD SHAW ("Candida").

THE susceptibilities of the poet might endure even the small red onions of the Morell household if they were boiled tender and served with a sauce of unthickened cream, seasoned with a dash of red pepper and a little chopped parsley.

DECEMBER 9TH

"The shepherdess who lives on salad."—GAY.

IF the shepherdess was as buxom and rosy as most of the old poets make her, she probably took care to have her salads substantial ones. This, a favorite with a physician renowned for his gastronomic wisdom, would answer her purpose: To a pint of cold, sliced potatoes add a tart apple sliced, a dozen slices of cold boiled beets, a few flakes of smoked herring, a small pickle sliced, a teaspoonful of capers, and a little chopped parsley. Mix with an ample quantity of mayonnaise dressing.

DECEMBER 10TH

"With corn to make your needy bread,
And give them life whom hunger starved half dead."—SHAKESPEARE ("Pericles").

A VERY nourishing corn bread is made with a cupful of cornmeal, two cupfuls of cold boiled rice, one cupful of milk, one egg, half a teaspoonful of salt, a tablespoonful of sugar, butter the size of an egg, and a teaspoonful of baking powder. Mix cornmeal, sugar, salt, and baking powder together; add the other ingredients after melting the butter and putting the rice through the colander. Bake half an hour.

DECEMBER 11TH

"And a large chestnut, the delicious meat
  Which Jove himself, were he a mouse, would eat."
                    —COWLEY ("Poems").

ROASTED chestnuts of the French or Italian variety are most satisfactory. Before cooking cut a slit in each nut; put them in a saucepan with just enough boiling water to cover them, boil thirty minutes. Drain and put in a hot oven for ten minutes and serve in a folded napkin. Pass salt with them. Care must be taken not to let the chestnuts cool after boiling before putting in the oven.

DECEMBER 12TH

"A Welsh Rabbit *à la cave au cidre.*"—THACKE-
RAY ("A Legend of the Rhine").

PUT in the blazer of a chafing-dish half a teacupful of Bass's ale and bring it to the boiling point. Add two pounds of rich American cheese, grated, stirring constantly; season with six teaspoonfuls of dry mustard and a shake or two of cayenne pepper. When it is smooth and creamy pour over hot toast. An egg beaten up and stirred in after the cheese has melted will prevent curdling, but if the cheese is of the right sort this will not be necessary, nor need the usual precaution of cooking the rabbit over hot water be taken.

DECEMBER 13TH

"Tea was made downstairs, biscuits and baked apples."—JANE AUSTEN ("Emma").

CORE and peel tart apples and bake in a porcelain-lined dish with half a cupful of water until they are transparent. Place them in a glass dish, fill the space left by the cores with whipped cream. Stick the apples closely with blanched almonds, and surround them with sugar and whipped cream flavored with maraschino.

DECEMBER 14TH

"Tea and coffee were there; a jug of water for Hewson."—ARTHUR HUGH CLOUGH ("The Bothie of Tober-na-Vuolich").

A CAFÉ frappé, very simple to prepare and satisfactory to partake of, is made by adding to one quart of black coffee one pint of whipped and sweetened cream. Turn into a freezer, pack in salt and ice, and allow it to stand for an hour and a half. Serve in tall glasses.

DECEMBER 15TH

"On one side of the table two green sauce-tureens, . . . were setting next to each other in a green dish; and on the other was a curried rabbit, in a brown suit, turned up with lemon."—CHARLES DICKENS ("Sketches by Boz").

SKIN the rabbit, clean it and divide in convenient pieces. Fry a slice of onion in butter; when brown put into the pan the pieces of rabbit, salted, peppered, and dredged with flour. Cook quickly for a few minutes, turning over often so that all parts may be seared. Cover with cold water, add parsley, sage, or any other herb whose flavor is liked, pepper and salt. When cooked tender take from the pan and keep hot while a gravy is made by adding butter, flour, catsup, and a dessertspoonful of curry-powder. Mushrooms are an improvement also. At the end add a glass of claret. Pour over the meat.

DECEMBER 16TH

"The beans and bacon set before 'em."—POPE.

TO prepare " Isle of Shoals Baked Beans " soak over night one quart of white beans in barely enough water to cover them; boil in same water; add to the water two tablespoonfuls of molasses. Put the beans in a deep earthen pot, place in the centre a generous piece of salt pork, with the rind, cut in strips, above the beans. Bake in a moderate heat for twenty-four hours. Two hours before serving give them a brisk heat. Serve hot in the pot. At the last baking add a little water from time to time if they seem too dry.

DECEMBER 17TH

"A little piece of salmon cut out of the fish's centre."—CHARLES READE ("It Is Never Too Late To Mend").

WASH and dry a slice of smoked salmon and broil slowly for twelve or fifteen minutes. Place it on a hot dish and spread over it a sauce made of a quarter of a cup of butter into which has been stirred half a teaspoonful of salt, a little paprika, and one tablespoonful each of chopped parsley and lemon juice.

DECEMBER 18TH

"They call for dates and quinces in the pastry." —SHAKESPEARE ("Romeo and Juliet").

TO make a date pudding soak in a cupful of milk a cupful of bread crumbs free from crusts; beat in two eggs, two tablespoonfuls of suet, chopped very fine; half a cupful of sugar, a saltspoonful each of salt and cinnamon, and a little nutmeg. Chop a cupful of dates and figs, dredge with a heaping tablespoonful of sifted flour and stir into the pudding. Beat hard for two or three minutes, pour into a well-buttered mould and steam for three hours. Eat with a hard sauce, well flavored with nutmeg and brandy or sherry.

DECEMBER 19TH

"Venison, the red and the roe, with mutton; and grouse succeeding." — ARTHUR HUGH CLOUGH "The Bothie of Tober-na-Vuolich").

CLEAN, wipe, and lard the legs and breast of grouse. Rub well with butter, dredge with flour, season with salt, and cook in a quick oven for thirty minutes if liked well done; twenty or less will be enough if liked rare.

DECEMBER 20TH

"I had rather have a handful or two of dried peas." — SHAKESPEARE ("Midsummer Night's Dream").

THE best use to put dried or split peas to is to make soup of them. Soak a cupful over night; put on to boil in three pints of fresh water, adding more as it boils away, so as to keep about three pints in the kettle. Stir often to keep from sticking to the sides of the kettle. When thoroughly soft put through a strainer and return to the fire. Stock, milk, or cream may be added to make it the consistency preferred. Add to the strained soup while boiling a tablespoonful of butter which has been melted and blended with one of flour; when it has all simmered ten minutes season with salt and pepper and serve. To many tastes this soup is greatly improved by adding to the water a ham-bone.

DECEMBER 21st

"Mushrooms, thought I, are better than these tasteless truffles, and so ordered a dish to try. You know what a Provençal sauce is?"—THACKERAY ("Memorials of Gormandising").

MOST American cooks do not know what a Provençal sauce is. Wash, peel, stem, and fry half a pound of fresh mushrooms. Remove from the pan. Put two or three raw mushrooms chopped fine, a clove of garlic, two chopped shallots, and two tablespoonfuls of olive-oil in the frying-pan, stir in while cooking a teaspoonful of flour, add half a pint of white wine and as much stock, two sprigs of parsley, one of thyme, half a bay leaf, salt and pepper, simmer about half an hour, strain, and pour over the fried mushrooms. If garlic is objected to, onion can be substituted, but garlic carefully used has the more delicate flavor of the two, and one that is slowly gaining favor in America.

224

DECEMBER 22D

"Certainly Savarin could not have lived in a country farm upon endives and mallows."—BULWER ("Parisians").

A MODERN confection in high favor among school girls and others is marshmallow penoche; to make it boil together two cupfuls of brown and one of white sugar, one cupful of milk, and butter the size of an egg; flavor with vanilla. Stir while cooking, which will take about twenty minutes; try by putting a little in water and if it balls readily it will be cooked enough, and you must then add a dozen soft marshmallow candies and beat thoroughly. Just before pouring into buttered plates, stir in a cupful of walnuts.

DECEMBER 23D

"At breakfast time when clippers yearly met,
Fill'd full of furmety, where dainty swum
The streaking sugar and the spotting plum."
—JOHN CLARE.

F URMETY was of old favored in having two days when it was especially appropriate to serve it— "Mothering-day" and Christmas—and for the tray of the invalid unable to eat the traditional plum pudding it was a not unacceptable substitute.

To two cupfuls of milk add four cupfuls of water and bring to the boiling point; add a level teaspoonful of salt and half a cupful of " pearl " or whole wheat. Stir constantly until it boils, then place in the upper part of a double boiler, the lower part of which is filled with boiling water, and cook for three hours. Serve with sugar, cinnamon, cream, and stewed prunes.

DECEMBER 24TH

"I went and got the best goose I could find (I don't think I ever saw a primer or ate more hearty myself), and had it roasted at three."—THACKERAY ("Dogs Have Their Day").

A GOOSE should be roasted longer and basted oftener than other poultry. Twenty-five minutes to the pound is none too long. For the stuffing mix bread crumbs and pulverized chestnuts, seasoned with salt and pepper. A green goose is one under four months old, and these are decidedly preferable to the older fowls. Gooseberry sauce is an appropriate accompaniment. Apple sauce is also orthodox.

"In half a minute Mrs. Cratchit entered—flushed but smiling proudly—with the pudding, like a speckled cannon-ball, so hard and firm, blazing in half of half-a-quartern of ignited brandy, and bedight with Christmas holly stuck into the top."— CHARLES DICKENS ("The Christmas Carol").

STONE one pound of raisins and add to them one-half gill of brandy, the grated rind of an orange and a lemon, one ounce each of candied lemon and orange peel and two of citron; one pound of clean currants, a quarter of a pound of almonds, blanched and pounded to a paste; a pound of suet, chopped fine and rubbed with four tablespoonfuls of flour; one teaspoonful of salt, a nutmeg, and one pound of fresh bread crumbs. Mix well and add a gill of sherry. Cover closely and stand in a cool place for a day. Just before boiling add eight eggs, well beaten, and enough cream to moisten, not enough to make soggy. Stir hard and pour into buttered moulds which have been dusted with flour; press pudding well into the mould to within two inches of the top. Put buttered paper on top, cover closely, and steam ten hours. It should be kept at least a month before using and steamed two more hours before serving. Do not open mould until ready to serve, when brandy should be poured over the pudding and lighted. Brandy sauce or rum sauce should be the accompaniment.

DECEMBER 26TH

"The poor little partridge was soon a heap of bones—a very little heap."—THACKERAY ("Memorials of Gormandising").

CUT the meat from the breast of a partridge, put the bone, together with the wings and legs, into a pan and cover with water. Add one small onion, a stalk of celery, a bit of whole mace, and a little salt and cayenne pepper, and boil until the liquor is reduced to a pint, then strain. Fry the breast meat in hot butter; after the meat is taken out of the frying pan add to the butter two tablespoonfuls of flour. Rub smooth; pour in the broth from the bones, boil until of a creamy consistency, pour over the meat and serve.

DECEMBER 27TH

"And as for the turkey and celery sauce, you should have seen how our host dispensed it!"— THACKERAY ("Memorials of Gormandising").

CELERY sauce gives to boiled turkey a delightful flavor. To prepare it heat in a saucepan a tablespoonful of butter, and as it melts slowly add a heaping tablespoonful of flour, stirring constantly. When thoroughly blended, pour in a pint of milk and keep steadily stirring until the sauce is smooth and thick; season with a saltspoonful of salt and a dash of pepper and the juice of half a lemon; stir in a cupful of chopped stewed celery, allow it to boil up once, and serve.

DECEMBER 28TH

"A cup of hot wine with not a drop of allaying Tyber in it."—SHAKESPEARE ("Coriolanus").

IN Roman days they may have served their wine hot, without a drop of water, but for a century or more the English rule for "mulled wine" calls for some "allaying" fluid. A large cupful of water should be boiled with a piece or two of stick-cinnamon and some grated nutmeg; take out the cinnamon, pour in a pint of port or sherry, add sugar to your taste, heat up once again, and it is ready.

DECEMBER 29TH

"Pray does anybody here hate cheese? I would be glad of a bit."—SWIFT.

A DISH which few men will hate is made by adding to one-quarter of a Camembert cheese a piece of butter the size of a large horse-chest-nut and a dash of paprika. Mix well with a pliable knife on a plate which has been rubbed with a clove of garlic. Remove the rind from the cheese before mixing with the butter.

DECEMBER 30TH

"Immense reduction in eggs—only one shilling each! ! !" — CHARLES READE ("It Is Never Too Late To Mend").

AT the price of a shilling apiece one may be sure eggs will be used singly, not in battalions, and the way to make the most of one would per-haps be to convert it into an eggnog. Beat the egg in a glass till very light

with a tiny pinch of salt; when light add
two teaspoonfuls of sugar and a glass of
sherry, grating a little nutmeg on top.
A very good temperance eggnog is made
by adding the juice of a lemon in place
of the sherry.

DECEMBER 31ST

"Christmas Day was at his elbow, plying him
with wassail - bowl, till he roared." — CHARLES
LAMB.

THE following recipe for wassail
punch is that used in one of the
oldest literary clubs of New York,
and the punch is served there on every
New Year's Eve. Put into two quarts
of boiling water a small bag of allspice
and leave it for two minutes. Take it
out and add to the water two quarts of
apple brandy and about a pound of
baked sweet apples cut in pieces. Serve
the punch very hot, keeping it over a
spirit-lamp to prevent its cooling. It
may be sweetened to taste by adding
more or less syrup made by boiling sugar
and water together, as for preserving
syrup.

INDEX

234